PRAISE FOR

Old Testament Survey I

"Nathan LeMaster puts in the hands of pastors and laity alike an accessible survey of the Old Testament. For each biblical book, he highlights the purpose, themes, and literary structure, all while noting key background information. This is a welcome resource for those wanting to read Holy Scripture with more care and detail."

— Ethan C. Jones
Don and Helen Bryant Chair of Old Testament
Associate Professor of Old Testament and Hebrew
New Orleans Baptist Theological Seminary

"Every Christian's spiritual journey should include many trips through the Old Testament. For both the first-time visitor and the seasoned traveler, Dr. Nathan LeMaster's volume on the Old Testament is an excellent travel guide!"

— Keith Essex
Emeritus Professor of Bible Exposition, The Master's Seminary

Titles in the Institute for the Christian Life Series

Published in 2023

Heaven and Hell: A Survey of the Biblical Doctrines of Personal Eschatology (Kevin Zuber)

The Forgotten Attributes of God: God's Nature and Why It Matters (Peter Sammons)

Old Testament Survey 1: Genesis to Esther (Nathan LeMaster)

Well Done: A Strategy for Life Stewardship (Reagan Rose)

Becoming a Worthy Reader: How to Read and Study the Bible (Kevin Zuber)

Coming in 2024 (tentative titles)

New Testament Survey 1 (Mark Zhakevich)

The Art of Biblical Discernment (Phil Johnson)

Biblical Gender and Sexuality (Mike Riccardi)

The Ordinary Church (John MacArthur)

Spiritual Gifts (Nate Busenitz)

Coming in 2025 (tentative titles)

Prayer (Carl Hargrove)

Old Testament Survey 2 (Nathan LeMaster)

Sanctification (Mike Riccardi)

Church Leadership (Kevin Zuber)

Offices of Christ (Peter Sammons)

Coming in 2026 (tentative titles)

Apologetics (Kevin Zuber)

Discipleship and Counseling (author TBD)

The Gospel of Grace (Peter Sammons)

The Trinity (Peter Sammons and Mike Riccardi)

New Testament Survey 2 (Mark Zhakevich)

BIBLE KNOWLEDGE

Old Testament Survey I

Genesis to Esther

NATHAN LEMASTER

CLC PUBLICATIONS
Fort Washington, PA 19034

Old Testament Survey I: Genesis to Esther
The Institute for the Christian Life Series

Published by CLC Publications

USA: P.O. Box 1449, Fort Washington, PA 19034
www.clcpublications.com

UK: Kingsway CLC Trust
Unit 5, Glendale Avenue, Sandycroft, Flintshire, CH5 2QP
www.equippingthechurch.com

ISBN (paperback): 978-1-61958-365-8
ISBN (ebook): 978-1-61958-377-1

Printed in the United States of America

Italics in Scripture quotations, if not original to the NASB, are the emphasis of the author.

Contents

Series Foreword

The Institute for the Christian Life Series

From the time the Lord called me to Grace Community Church, I have had two primary goals: to preach the Word of God faithfully (2 Tim. 4:2) and to entrust the truth to faithful men (2:2). In keeping with those priorities, The Master's Seminary has played a key role in training future pastors to handle the Word accurately and defend its truth boldly. These Master's men have gone out to serve and shepherd churches across the nation and around the world.

Several years ago, to assist these faithful pastors in their shepherding work, the seminary created a lay-training program, comprised of online video courses. The Institute for the Christian Life (originally called the Institute for Church Leadership) is designed to train lay people in four fundamental categories: Bible Knowledge, Sound Doctrine, Christian Living, and Shepherding Care.

The ICL is designed to bring biblical training, theological instruction, and practical ministry into the pew and the living room—making these indispensable tools accessible to believers at all levels of spiritual maturity and church leadership. This book series complements those online courses, as an aid for small group discussion and individual study.

My prayer for you as you read this book, and engage with the corresponding video content through the ICL, is that you would grow in the grace and knowledge of the Lord Jesus Christ. As the apostle Paul expressed in Ephesians 1:18–19, "*I pray* that the eyes of your heart may be enlightened, so that you will know what is the hope of His calling, what are the riches of the glory of His inheritance in the saints, and what is the surpassing greatness of His power toward us who believe."

John MacArthur
Pastor, Grace Community Church, Sun Valley, California
Chancellor, The Master's University and Seminary

Editorial Preface

Dr. Nathan LeMaster (PhD, Cambridge) serves as Assistant Professor of Old Testament at The Master's Seminary. He brings the first volume in a series of books dedicated to Bible Survey of the Old Testament. Many, even within the church, often underestimate the importance of the Old Testament. Too often, believers neglect the rich history found in the Old Testament because they deem it to be impractical or irrelevant.

B. B. Warfield once said, "The Old Testament may be likened to a chamber richly furnished but dimly lighted; the introduction of light brings into it nothing which was not in it before; but it brings out into clearer view much of what is in it but was only dimly or even not at all perceived before. The mystery of the Trinity is not revealed in the Old Testament; but the mystery of the Trinity underlies the Old Testament revelation, and here and there almost comes into view. Thus the Old Testament revelation of God is not corrected by the fuller revelation that follows it, but only perfected, extended and enlarged."

The richness of the Old Testament is best understood and appreciated by New Testament believers, for the Old Testament reveals Christ. The Old Testament doesn't just "point forward" to Christ; it reveals Him. This book covers the major themes and events of the books of Genesis through Esther: tracing the major developments and rich history, chapter-by-chapter, highlighting unique and important features to help believers in their own personal study of each book. Whether you have time-tested experience in ministry, or you're a new believer, we expect this book will provide both the rigor and refreshment necessary to help you in your labor for the Lord.

Peter Sammons, PhD
Faculty Associate in Systematic Theology
The Master's Seminary

INTRODUCTION

OLD TESTAMENT SCHOLARS are sometimes portrayed as having a chip on their shoulder. Normally, the New Testament receives most of the time in the pulpit. Most Christians spend their devotional time in the New Testament. Churchgoers know several of the Old Testament stories, such as Daniel in the Lion's Den, the flood, and the Ten Commandments. But when asked how the Mosaic law relates to the Christian, or what significance Second Samuel 7 and the Davidic covenant had on Jesus' ministry, most churchgoers cannot speak at length.

This often leaves Old Testament scholars murmuring that the Old Testament, after all, does make up 80 percent of the Bible, and there are thirty-nine books in the Old Testament compared with twenty-seven in the New Testament. They may also mumble that people should start with first things first.

The intention of this book is not to guilt you into reading the laws of the sacrificial system for your devotions. You do not gain extra credit with God because you actually made it through Leviticus in your yearly Bible reading plan without giving up. The purpose of this book is to show the relevance, the intricacy, and the intention of the Old Testament. The heart of this book is to reignite a passion for Old Testament studies because, honestly, much has been left in mothballs that shouldn't be there.

It is also important to recognize the relationship between the Old and New Testaments. They are often pitted against each other. In fact, you may have heard some Christians who speak about the "God of the Old Testament" as though He were different from the New Testament. How can the God who commanded the destruction of the Canaanite nations be the same God who sent His one and only Son to die on behalf of sinful man? Didn't God strike Uzzah dead for just touching the ark of the covenant when it was teetering over the mud? What kind of God commands a nation of people not to wear clothing woven of two types of material? Can't Christians get by just fine without having to delve into all of that Old Testament stuff?

The answer is no. When the Old Testament is ignored, we Christians miss out on more than we realize. The New Testament assumes that the reader has read the Old Testament. Not only do New Testament writers quote the Old Testament, but much is assumed in the New Testament that has its foundation in the Old Testament. For example, Matthew starts with the genealogy of Jesus. The only way to understand his intention in doing so is to examine the genealogies of Genesis and the rest of the Old Testament. Both John the Baptist's and Jesus' first sermons included, "The kingdom of heaven is at hand" (see Matt. 3:2; 4:17). It is assumed that the reader knows what they referred to based on the teaching of the Old Testament.

Not only is much assumed in the New Testament, but examining the Old Testament brings a wonderful joy. King David, in Psalm 19:7–8, said about the Pentateuch,[1] "The law of the LORD is perfect, restoring the soul / . . . The precepts of the LORD are right, rejoicing the heart / The commandment of the LORD is pure, enlightening the eyes."[2] David said also in Psalm 119:77, "Your law is my delight."

This book is intended to help you replace any feeling of drudgery when you open the Old Testament with a desire and a longing to understand the Old Testament, the God who is described in the Old Testament, and the relationship of the Christian to the Old Testament.

THE ORGANIZATION OF THE OLD TESTAMENT

As any good Old Testament scholar will say, "First things first." We must begin with an overview of the Old Testament to show how it all fits together. Our English Bibles are divided into thirty-nine books. This division is based on the Septuagint, the Greek translation of the Old Testament.

The organization of the books is somewhat different in the Hebrew Old Testament. The books and the text are the same as the Hebrew; they are just organized differently in the English. In the Hebrew, the Old Testament begins with Genesis, Exodus, Leviticus, Numbers, and Deuteronomy. This

1 The *Pentateuch* is a Greek word for the first five books of the Bible: Genesis, Exodus, Leviticus, Numbers, and Deuteronomy. In Judaism, the same five books are referred to as the *Torah*. The Torah is also a word that is used by the Old Testament to speak about the first five books of the Old Testament. Torah is one of the Hebrew words for instruction/teaching.

2 All Biblical quotations are taken from the NASB 1995, unless otherwise noted. At times, the name of God, *Yahweh,* will be used in brackets where the NASB only puts "LORD" in small-capped letters to designate that it is the name *Yahweh.*

is the first major division, and these first five books are foundational to all that comes after them.

The second division of the Hebrew Old Testament is "The Prophets," which is called the *Nevi'im* in Hebrew. The organization of these books is Joshua, Judges, Samuel, Kings, Isaiah, Jeremiah, Ezekiel, and The Twelve. The books that are divided by first and second (like First Kings and Second Kings) are actually one complete book. So First Samuel and Second Samuel in our English Bibles, are really just the book of Samuel. Again, it is the same text, just organized differently. The same is true for Kings and Chronicles. The Twelve is also understood as a compendium of books which includes Hosea, Joel, Amos, Obadiah, Jonah, Micah, Nahum, Habakkuk, Zephaniah, Haggai, Zechariah, and Malachi.

The third division of the Hebrew Old Testament is "The Writings," called the *Ketuvim* in Hebrew. The order of these books is Psalms, Proverbs, Job, Song of Solomon, Ruth, Lamentations, Qoheleth (also called Ecclesiastes), Esther, Daniel, Ezra, Nehemiah, and Chronicles. Much like First and Second Samuel, First and Second Kings, and First and Second Chronicles, Ezra and Nehemiah are linked together. Though understood as two separate books, they are still thought of as linked.

We can organize the Old Testament books in several ways. We have seen the different ordering of the books in the Septuagint, in contrast to the Hebrew ordering of the books. But we can also make additional groupings. For example, Job, Ecclesiastes, and Proverbs make up the "Wisdom Literature" books. We can also study the "historical" books, which include Joshua, Judges, Samuel, Kings, Chronicles, Ezra, Nehemiah, Ruth, and Esther. This first volume on the Old Testament will examine the Pentateuch and the historical books. The second volume will cover the rest of the Old Testament.

What is important to recognize about the Old Testament organization is the reliance of all books on the Pentateuch. These first five books of the Old Testament are always at the beginning of the Old Testament. This is because they form the foundation of all that comes after. The main purpose of the Prophetic Books is to show how Israel responded to the Pentateuch on a national level. The Writings have a different focus, asking how the individual should respond to the Pentateuch. The Writings such as Psalms, Proverbs, and Ruth, are usually easier for Christians to read, because they focus on a person's response to the Pentateuch. The bridge to reach the intention of David in the Psalms is much shorter than the bridge to reach the intention of Ezekiel, for example.

Study questions:

1. Which parts of the Bible do you find most challenging to read and apply to your life? Why might this be, and how does understanding the organization and bigger picture of the Bible help us with these more challenging portions?

2. What is the relationship between the Pentateuch and the rest of the Old Testament?

3. Does the Pentateuch have a main theme? If so, how would you describe it?

4. If there were a central passage to the Pentateuch, what would it be? And how does that help you understand the rest of the Pentateuch?

5. Why does it matter how the Bible is organized?

6. How could you adapt your current reading plan to begin to expose yourself more to the Old Testament on a daily basis?

1

GENESIS

THE ENTIRE BIBLE IS inspired and inerrant, which means each of the biblical books is an important and necessary component to the whole of the Bible. But there are also pinnacle books—books that stand at the top of the mountain. Genesis is such a book. Genesis lays the foundation for all we know about God, the nature of humans, the promise of salvation, and the life of faith.

But Genesis can also be difficult to understand. It is full of wondrous stories that seem, at times, to be far removed from the world we see around us. It can be hard to imagine the entire world deluged in water, people who lived hundreds of years, or all of humankind uniting to build a tower.

At times, Genesis makes unusual statements with no further explanation. An example would be Genesis 5:24, "Enoch walked with God; and he was not, for God took him." The reader of Genesis might be left with unanswered questions in his mind. Where did God take him? Did Enoch die like the others in chapter 5? What was God's purpose in taking him?

We might even point to the creation account as another example. Why were only two chapters dedicated to the creation of the universe? Why was there not more explanation? Could we perhaps trade some of the genealogy chapters for more chapters on how God created the world?

We must go back to our original statement that the Bible is inspired and inerrant. That means each passage in Genesis is exactly how God intended it. No more, no less. There is intention behind all that is mentioned, and all that is excluded. While we may want more explanation or insight, Genesis gives us what God wants us to know.

An overview study of Genesis requires three areas of study. First, we need to understand the structure of the book. Identifying the structure or organization of the book will shed light on the authorial intention.

Second, we need to determine the purpose of Genesis. Each biblical book has a unique purpose for being included in the canon of Scripture.

Third, we need to examine the themes that run through the book. Every book of the Bible has several themes. But Genesis holds a unique place at the start of the Bible. The themes that we see in Genesis will be picked up and carried along through the rest of Scripture.

STRUCTURE

Structure and organization are important to understand in each biblical book. These are important because each author organized his book in order to highlight, emphasize, or outline the key concepts and themes.

Additionally, at times we can see several different structures at work in a single book. This is the case with Genesis. Even after an initial read through the book, the reader notes the shift in narrative between chapters 11 and 12. Chapters 1–11 speak to the creation, the development of culture and civilization, the judgment of the flood, and the rebellion of humanity in the Tower of Babel. These stories each reference humanity as a whole. Indeed, there are individual characters, such as Noah, Eve, Seth, and Nimrod. But the focus of chapters 1–11 is on humanity, its inception, rebellion, and judgment.

Chapter 12 starts with a new focus: Abraham. From this point until the end of Genesis, the patriarchs are in view. We can point to the structure of Genesis as:

1. Chapters 1–11: Primeval History
2. Chapters 12–50: Patriarchal History

However, Genesis has an additional structure that we should not miss, and it is rooted in all of those genealogies. We might wonder about the usefulness of the genealogies. Honestly, how many Christians do their daily devotions in the genealogies? But we must remember our first premise, that the Bible is inspired and inerrant, meaning that everything included in Scripture is profitable and useful (2 Tim. 3:16). The genealogies are no exception to this. This structure of the genealogies actually starts in Genesis 2:4, "This is the account of the heavens and the earth when they were created." The word for "account" is actually the Hebrew word for "genealogy/generation." The Hebrew word is pronounced *toledot*. This *toledot* formula shows us another structure to Genesis.

Genesis 2:4—"This is the *[toledot]* of the heavens and the earth when they were created."

Genesis 5:1—"This is the book of the *[toledot]* of Adam."

Genesis 6:9 —"These are the records of the *[toledot]* of Noah."

Genesis 10:1—"Now these are the records of the *[toledot]* of Shem, Ham, and Japheth, the sons of Noah."

Genesis 10:32—"These are the families of the sons of Noah, according to their *[toledot]*, by their nations; and out of these the nations were separated on the earth after the flood."

Genesis 11:10—"These are the records of the *[toledot]* of Shem."

Genesis 11:27—"Now these are the records of the *[toledot]* of Terah. Terah became the father of Abram, Nahor and Haran."

Genesis 25:12—"Now these are the records of the *[toledot]* of Ishmael."

Genesis 25:19—"Now these are the records of the *[toledot]* of Isaac, Abraham's son."

Genesis 36:1—"Now these are the records of the *[toledot]* of Esau."

Genesis 37:2—"These are the records of the *[toledot]* of Jacob."

Each time a new *toledot* was given, it opened a new story line. The focus narrowed throughout Genesis, starting with the heavens and the earth in general, then moving to Adam, to Noah, to Shem, to Abraham, and eventually to Isaac and Jacob. In a similar way to the division between Genesis 1–11 and Genesis 12–50, the focus narrowed from all of humanity down to Abraham, Isaac, and finally Jacob.

Ultimately, the focus would narrow to the twelve sons of Jacob, with Judah rising above the rest. Other books continued to carry this line. The books of Ruth and Samuel, for example, would narrow the focus even more from Judah to the house of David. Matthew would pick up on this focus and begin his gospel with a genealogy that ends with Christ Jesus.[1] Both of these structures that are seen in Genesis point to the purpose of Genesis.

Purpose

Each Bible book has a unique place in the whole canon of Scripture, and each book has a specific purpose that is distinct from all other biblical books. One way to help us distinguish the purpose of one book from another is to create a purpose statement for each book. Especially for a book like Genesis, it can be difficult to fit all the components into a single purpose

1 Much can be said about this narrowing of focus seen in the genealogies. We must also note the genealogies of those who are not in Christ's line. We see examples with the genealogy of Ishmael and Esau. These also serve an important function, showing God's care for all the nations (see also Psalm 67 and the emphasis on all nations following Yahweh).

statement. However, key themes and motifs rise to the surface throughout Genesis, which can be reflected in a purpose statement.

> **Genesis purpose statement:** The sovereign God of creation chose to bless the rebellious human race through Abraham and his seed.

Not all themes of Genesis can be reflected in a single purpose statement. Themes not included in this statement are: God's promise of the land of Canaan to Abraham, God's gift of a covenant, and God's punishment of rebellion. But this statement gets to the heart of the intention of Genesis. God is sovereign, having all power and authority over His creation. The God of creation is the same God of Abraham; there is no other god. Humankind rebelled and attempted to throw off the yoke of God's authority. And God selected Abraham and his descendants, through whom He would bring the promised Redeemer.

Themes

It is difficult to speak to all of the themes running through the book of Genesis. The other sixty-five books of the Bible come after Genesis and assume that the reader has read Genesis. The other sixty-five books will carry on themes that are established in Genesis, such as the image of God in humans, the authority of God in creation, God's choice of Abraham and his descendants, etc. For the sake of conciseness and clarity, the following section will deal with four major themes in Genesis: (1) God's sovereignty, (2) The work of creation, (3) The cycle of sin, judgment, and mercy, and (4) God's choice of Abraham.

God's Sovereignty

Genesis established what we know about God's character. Through this simple sentence, "In the beginning God created the heavens and the earth," God was established as the authority. The Creator/creature distinction was set in stone. God created not only the physical substance of the universe, but He also created the immaterial. This would include the social structures that were put in place (e.g., marriage and the family) as well as the rights of His creatures. The one who created had authority to determine what the rights of the creation would be.

Or perhaps a better way to put it: You do not have any rights outside of what God has ordained. There is no appeal to a higher authority, no law outside of God. In fact, when Adam and Eve sinned, they were seeking power and knowledge outside of what God had permitted for them. The serpent tempted with, "You will be like God, knowing good and evil" (Gen. 3:5). This step outside of what God permitted cast humanity into sin. Even after the rebellion, God's sovereign sustaining power remained.

Creation in seven days should also be understood in conjunction with God's sustaining power. God not only created *ex nihilo* (out of nothing), but God also sustained the creation in every moment. Colossians 1:17 clearly states that by the power of Jesus Christ, all things hold together.

It is false thinking to see God creating the universe and then stepping back to let it run itself. This leads to a clearer understanding of God's grace to humankind, even after the fall. Adam and Eve, attempting to step outside of God's sovereign authority, found themselves relationally separated from God, condemned by their sin. But God's sovereign power to sustain them did not cease after their rebellion. God continued to sustain His creation, providing time for repentance.

God's sovereignty was not only on display in Genesis through the creation, but also throughout the entire book. We see a wonderful example in the story of Joseph. Moses, the writer of Genesis, intended for his readers to see that God sovereignly worked in all things.

Joseph, after being sold into slavery by his brothers because of their jealousy, landing in Egypt as a slave, rising to become a chief slave in the house of a powerful man, being thrown into prison because of a false accusation against him, and finally being exalted to be the second most powerful man in Egypt, told his brothers, "As for you, you meant evil against me, *but* God meant it for good, in order to bring about this present result, to preserve many people alive" (Gen. 50:20). In Genesis, humans were portrayed as scheming and plotting, but God was ultimately in control, to bring about His plan of redemption.

The Creation

The work of creation was mentioned regarding God's sovereignty. But much more should be said about creation.

Creation not only shows God's sovereignty and ultimate authority, but it also explains the place of humanity within the creation. The nature of being human, the inalienable rights of each human being, and the effects of sin on humankind are all seen in just the first three chapters of Genesis.

We should not underestimate the importance of the image of God in humans. God created light the first day, the atmosphere the second day, the dry land and vegetation the third day, the stars and planets and moons the fourth day, the fish and the birds the fifth day, and for the sixth day, God made the land animals and Adam. Adam was the crown jewel of the creation. Genesis emphasized that Adam was created unique from the rest of the animals. Both Adam and Eve were created "in the image of God" (Gen. 1:27).

The image of God in humans is not easily defined. Ecclesiastes 3:11 says that God has placed eternity in the heart of humans, the ability to think outside of the constant physical cycle of life, toil, and death.

We might also point to the ability to speak a language as a clear separation between humans and animals. Animals have forms of rudimentary communication, but only human language has the capacity to communicate any thought, feeling, desire, or intention. The gift of language allows people to communicate metaphorically, abstractly, and even theologically.

We might also point to the image of God as the everlasting immaterial nature of man. Animals have a beginning and an ending. We have a beginning, but our souls will continue on after the death of the physical body. The image of God in humans has far reaching implications. But an aspect we can clearly see born out of the image of God is that each human being has subsequent rights.

Genesis 9:6 says that because man is created in the image of God, whoever murders a human being must be put to death. Murder is an assault not only on the victim, but it is also an assault on the God whom that person represents. It is as if humans are ambassadors for God within creation.

A necessary hierarchy is built within creation. God, who is the ultimate authority, has delegated authority within His creation. Humans have inalienable rights through being created in the image of God to act as representatives within the creation. Humanity is charged with the care of God's creation. But the rebellion of man has brought about a schism in the creation. What should be in harmony is now in opposition. Authority becomes tyranny, relationship becomes manipulation, and the bounty of God's creation becomes an occasion for greed and obsession. What was perfect and beautiful has now become twisted by the rebellion of humanity.

Sin, Judgment, and Mercy

We see a consistent pattern of sin, judgment, and mercy throughout Genesis. Adam and Eve rebelled, they were judged by being cast out of the garden of Eden, but God showed them mercy by covering their nakedness and shame. Cain murdered his brother Abel, he was exiled, but God showed him mercy by placing a mark on him so that no one would kill him.

The wickedness of man spread on the earth so that "every intent of the thoughts of his heart was only evil continually" (Gen. 6:5), God judged by sending a worldwide flood, but God showed mercy by preserving Noah and his family in the ark. The cities of Sodom and Gomorrah were completely corrupt and wicked, God sent fire from heaven to destroy the cities, but God showed mercy by preserving Lot and his two daughters.

Again and again in Genesis we see this cycle. God judged rebellion and sin, but then He also showed mercy, not bringing complete destruction upon His creation.

This mercy is also seen in the establishment of two covenants in Genesis. Exodus further develops the understanding of a covenant. But covenants are also key for understanding Genesis. The covenant that God made with Noah is the first in Genesis. The second is the covenant with Abram.[2]

The covenant with Noah was the only covenant that God made with the entire creation. Genesis 9:9–10 says that God made a covenant with Noah, his descendants, and "every living creature."

Each biblical covenant has different components. The Noahic covenant is a covenant of time. Through the Noahic covenant, God gives His creation time—time to repent, time to return to Him. God promises that He will not again destroy the entire earth with a flood, no matter how wicked humans become on the earth. God will still give wicked time. This kindness has been seen throughout history, up until this day. However, without a way of redemption, time does not fix the problem. The Abrahamic covenant is the entry gate into redemption.

God's Choice of Abraham

A major theme that starts in Genesis 12 and runs through the rest of the book is the Abrahamic covenant. This covenant is reemphasized with Isaac and with Jacob as well.[3] There are three components to the Abrahamic covenant:

1. God will make Abraham into a great nation (Gen. 15:5).
2. God will give Abraham the land of Canaan (15:7).
3. God promises that through Abraham all humankind will be blessed. (12:3).

---

2 In Hebrew the name Abram means "exalted father." God changed Abram's name to Abraham which means "father of a multitude."

3 See especially Genesis 26:1–5 and 35:9–12.

2

Exodus

As the Pentateuch progresses, time slows down. The events in Genesis start at the beginning of creation and end with Jacob bringing his entire family to Egypt, which would have been c. 1875 BC. That span of time is a few thousand years. The events of Exodus cover a few hundred years, from Jacob going down into Egypt (c. 1875 BC) to the building of the Tabernacle (c. 1445 BC). Leviticus and Numbers cover forty years of Israel's history, and Deuteronomy covers thirty days of Israel's history.

More chapters are devoted to increased description and explanation as we near the end of the Pentateuch. Whereas, in Genesis, the first eleven chapters covered a few thousand years of history, Exodus devotes eighteen chapters to the laws and regulations for Israel, including the building of the Tabernacle. This is with specific intention. We should not gloss over the chapters that explain the laws given to Israel. This will also be true in Leviticus, Numbers, and Deuteronomy. We can learn much about God's nature, His mercy, man's sin, atonement, redemption, and many other key theological tenets. First, let's examine the structure to understand the purpose of Exodus more clearly.

Structure

The structure of Exodus can be seen in terms of the Israelites' location.

Exodus 1:1–Exodus 15:21	The Israelites in Egypt
Exodus 15:22–Exodus 40	The Israelites at Sinai

This change in location is the backdrop for the dramatic story of Israel's deliverance from bondage in Egypt. And in this story, we are first introduced to Moses, a man whose character will be developed throughout the rest of the Pentateuch. During this story line, Moses will change from being a brazen murderer to a man of godly humility (Num. 12:3). Additional substructure can be seen within these two major sections of Exodus:

Exodus 1:1–4:31	The oppression of Israel and the introduction of a deliverer
Exodus 5:1–15:21	The deliverance of Israel from bondage in Egypt
Exodus 15:22–18:27	Israel travels to Mount Sinai
Exodus 19:1–24:18	The making of the Mosaic covenant
Exodus 25:1–31:18	The revelation of the Tabernacle
Exodus 32:1–34:35	The breaking and renewal of the Mosaic covenant
Exodus 35:1–40:38	The completion of the Tabernacle

Purpose

The purpose of Exodus is seen in the structure of the book. God is the cause of Israel's movement from Egypt to Sinai. This is the start of the fulfillment of God's promises to Abraham. Even the first few verses of Exodus show this. Exodus 1:1–6 describes those seventy people who went into Egypt with Jacob. Exodus 1:7 says Israel grew exceedingly and became a numerous people, pointing to God's promise to Abraham that he would be the father of a great nation.

God had chosen Israel, and God would redeem Israel, inextricably placing His name on them. The purpose is parallel with the structure:

> **Exodus purpose statement:** Yahweh redeems Israel from bondage in Egypt and enters into a covenant with them at Mount Sinai.

Themes

The Name Yahweh

An important statement about the name of God is found in Exodus 6:2–3, "God spoke further to Moses and said to him, 'I am [Yahweh]; and I appeared to Abraham, Isaac, and Jacob, as God Almighty, but by My name, [Yahweh], I did not make Myself known to them.'"

However, Abraham did use the name *Yahweh*. Genesis 15:2 states, "But Abram said, 'O Lord God, what will you give me, since I am childless, and the heir of my house is Eliezer of Damascus?'"

The word translated as God in this verse is Yahweh. So what can Exodus 6:2–3 mean? It is not as though Moses, the author of both Genesis and Exodus, forgot that the name Yahweh was used before Exodus 6:2–3. The implication is not that there is a contradiction here but that God is saying something about Himself and His relationship to Israel.

Abraham saw God as the almighty One. Abraham saw God provide a ram in place of his son Isaac on Mount Moriah in Genesis 22. Abraham called that place "[Yahweh] will provide" (Gen. 22:14).

Abraham saw the power of God when he opened the womb of Sarah, a ninety-year-old woman who had never had children. Abraham, Isaac, and Jacob knew God as the all-powerful One who created the heavens and the earth. And Abraham, Isaac, and Jacob knew of the name Yahweh. But in Exodus 6:2–3, God promised that He would reveal Himself in a new way to the nation of Israel. They would know Him through His covenant name, Yahweh. You might even say that they would now be on a first name basis.

Names are important throughout the Bible. This goes back to creation itself. The One who creates has the authority to give the name. In the Old Testament, names were not arbitrary or necessarily given because they sounded pretty. A name described and defined the person.

The basis for Adam's name was the Hebrew word for dirt. Adam gave his wife the name Eve because her name means "life-giver." Lamech named his son Noah, meaning "rest," because he hoped his son would "give us rest from our work" (Gen. 5:29). Nimrod's name meant "rebel," which was fitting for this wicked, violent man. God renamed Abraham because He would make him a father of a multitude. Abraham named his son Isaac, which means laughter, because of the laughter surrounding the story of his birth. Jacob received his name because from birth he was a usurper.

The importance of names is seen throughout the Bible. Even the Holy Spirit commanded Joseph and Mary to name their son Jesus, salvation, because He would save His people from their sins (Matt. 1:21).

Yahweh is not a name that was given to God. No one has authority over God, and so no one can give God His name. God chooses to reveal His name to His people.

What is also important to see in Exodus is that God was inextricably linking His name with Israel. Through the powerful works that God did on Israel's behalf, He associated Himself with Israel. When Israel acted wickedly, this is a blight against the name of God.

In Exodus 32:10, after Israel created the golden calf, God's anger burned against Israel because of their idolatry. Moses interceded on Israel's behalf and appealed to God not to destroy the people because all of the nations had linked Yahweh with Israel. Israel's destruction would negate the promises God made to Abraham. But Israel's continued obstinance tarnished the name of Yahweh. This tension would be seen again, especially in Leviticus and Numbers.

Additionally, we also see this theme of Yahweh's name in the Ten Commandments. The third commandment specifically used the name Yahweh, "You shall not take the name of [Yahweh], your God in vain, for [Yahweh] will not leave him unpunished who takes His name in vain" (Exod. 20:7).

Yahweh inaugurated the relationship with Israel in Exodus by revealing Himself to them by His covenant name. And Yahweh expected His people to reverence His name. This theme not only runs throughout the Pentateuch but is also seen through the entire Old Testament. Ezekiel reminded Israel that they eluded destruction only because of the name of Yahweh. Speaking of Israel, Ezekiel said,

> They rebelled against Me and were not willing to listen to Me; they did not cast away the detestable things of their eyes, nor did they forsake the idols of Egypt. Then I resolved to pour out My wrath on them, to accomplish My anger against them in the midst of the land of Egypt. But I acted for the sake of My name, that it should not be profaned in the sight of the nations among whom they *lived*, in whose sight I made Myself known to them by bringing them out of the land of Egypt. (Ezek. 20:8–9)

Because of the name—we could even say the glory—of Yahweh, Israel was not destroyed.

Redemption

Another theme in Exodus that is tied with the name of Yahweh is the concept of redemption. Not only did Yahweh place His name on Israel, but Yahweh purchased Israel. Israel was moving from one master to another, from the Egyptians to Yahweh. Exodus 6:6 says, "Say, therefore, to the sons of Israel, 'I am [Yahweh], and I will bring you out from under the burdens of the Egyptians, and I will deliver you from their bondage. I will also redeem you with an outstretched arm and with great judgments.'"

These great judgments ultimately culminated in the death of all first-born in Egypt, both animals and people.

We must remember that Israel was not any more righteous than the Egyptians. God was not bringing them out of the land of Egypt because they were holier. In fact, the Israelites worshipped the same idols as the Egyptians. Ezekiel 20:8, quoted above, explains that the Israelites did not forsake the idols of Egypt, even after they were delivered from Egypt. Not only did they create a golden calf in Exodus 32, but they carried around their idols, which they took with them from Egypt, even until the days of Joshua (Josh. 24:23). Israel was not redeemed out of Egypt because they were more righteous than the Egyptians. They were moving from one master to another, and the payment they owed was the firstborn.

God spared the firstborn of Israel from death. Because of this, God required all the firstborn of Israel to be dedicated to Him. Before Israel even left Egypt, God commanded Moses to inform the people that all of the firstborn of Israel belonged to Him, both animals and people.

Exodus 13:11–16 explains that every firstborn needed to be consecrated to the Lord. The Israelites were required to sacrifice the firstborn of their clean animals.[1] An unclean animal was not to be sacrificed, but the owner was to sacrifice a clean animal in its place, to redeem that animal. Otherwise, the unclean animal would be put to death.

All firstborn children had to be redeemed. If the parents did not want the child to be dedicated to lifelong service for Yahweh, then they were required to make a payment. By the time we get to Numbers 3:40–51, Yahweh exchanged all firstborn from every tribe of Israel for the entire tribe of Levi. The Levites became the payment of Israel's redemption out of Egypt. The Levites were not given allotted land as the other tribes of Israel, but they were dedicated to temple service for life.

Redemption is an important theme in Exodus. Israel did not earn their deliverance from Egypt. They were just as wicked as the Egyptians. However, God, based on His promises to Abraham, Isaac, and Jacob, redeemed Israel from Egypt. Israel changed masters from the Egyptians to Yahweh. The price to pay was all firstborn, eventually traded for the entire tribe of Levi in Numbers 3.

Covenant

We also saw the theme of covenant in Genesis, but it is further developed in Exodus. At the heart of the Abrahamic covenant are the promises that God made to Abraham. Abraham demonstrated his faith, trusting that God would do what He had promised. But no requirements were given for the

1 Further explanation will be given about the distinction between clean and unclean in the chapter on Leviticus.

Abrahamic covenant. God simply promised that He would make Abraham into a great nation, give him the land of Canaan, and bless the nations through Abraham. The Abrahamic covenant can be seen as a one-sided covenant. God simply stipulated how He would act toward Abraham.

This is also seen in the Noahic covenant. The promises that God made to Noah, his descendants, and all creation did not have any stipulations. In fact, the main point of the Noahic covenant was that God was granting time to His creation, no matter what they did. Humankind was unable to break the Noahic covenant, no matter how wicked they became. God promised that He would not destroy the world again by a flood, allotting time for His creatures to repent rather than be destroyed in their rebellion.

The Mosaic covenant stands in contrast to the Abrahamic and Noahic covenants. First, the Israelites were required to commit to the covenant. Exodus 19:1–9 was the agreement between Yahweh and the people of Israel. This occurred immediately after the people arrived at Mount Sinai.

In Exodus 19:1–6, Yahweh again pointed to the fact that He had inextricably tied His name with Israel. If Israel obeyed, then they would be blessed. Israel's answer to the stipulations is recounted in Exodus 19:7–8, "So Moses came and called the elders of the people, and set before them all these words which [Yahweh] had commanded him. All the people answered together and said, 'All that [Yahweh] has spoken we will do!'"

Notice that the text says that all Israel answered, and the people all answered together. The nation was in agreement, and they entered into the covenant with Yahweh. Israel was legally bound to Yahweh, but it only took Israel a few days before they broke the covenant by fashioning the golden calf and worshipping a false god.

The ramifications of the Mosaic covenant will be seen throughout the Pentateuch and beyond. However, it is important to ask, "Why did God enter into a covenant at all with Israel? What is the purpose of a covenant?"

In simple terms, a covenant establishes the boundaries of a relationship. The covenant stipulates how each party will act for the benefit of the relationship. This is seen in human covenants such as marriage, where both the husband and wife promise to each other how they will act and treat the other. Some covenants can be unilateral, such as the Abrahamic covenant, in which only one party, God, is required to fulfill the stipulations of the covenant. And because "God is not a man, that He should lie," (Num. 23:19) the fulfillment of the covenant is certain.

In contrast, the Mosaic covenant, like a marriage covenant, can be violated. The people of Israel quickly accepted the terms, not fully considering what it meant to be a sinful people who were entering a covenant with a holy God. The boundaries to the relationship between God and Israel is a key aspect of the Mosaic covenant. This set the stage for the sacrificial system outlined in Leviticus. But it was also seen at the outset of Israel's time at Mount Sinai. Exodus 19:12 states, "You shall set bounds for the people all around, saying, 'Beware that you do not go up on the mountain or touch the border of it; whoever touches the mountain shall surely be put to death.'"

A great tension existed because Israel and God had a covenant relationship, but the holy presence of God only brings death to sinful people. This is why the Tabernacle is vital to understanding Exodus and God's relationship with Israel.

The Tabernacle

Unfortunately for many Christians, around the start of the Tabernacle description in Exodus, the annual Bible reading challenge starts to seem daunting. Genesis has relatable characters, and Exodus 1–20 contains amazing stories that grip the attention. But around Exodus 25, many Old Testament readers start to question why the Tabernacle—and all the rules and regulations surrounding it—are important.

The Tabernacle and the Mosaic covenant go hand in hand. Just as the Mosaic covenant established the boundaries of the relationship between God and Israel, the Tabernacle physically represented those boundaries. The Tabernacle had an outer court, an inner court, and the holy of holies. Not just anyone could enter the outer court. Even fewer were allowed in the inner court. And only one person, the high priest who was properly cleansed, could enter the holy of holies, and that only once a year.

The rules for gaining entry into the Tabernacle were for the protection of Israel, not for the protection of Yahweh. Those who took these stipulations lightly were killed, as we shall see in Leviticus 10 with the deaths of Nadab and Abihu.

The blueprints for the Tabernacle were given in Exodus, and it was to be constructed in an exact fashion. The sections of the Tabernacle could all be quickly deconstructed and stored for transport. Those elements which could not be touched, such as the ark of the covenant, had golden rings through which wooden poles were inserted so the Levites could hoist it on their shoulders.

3

Leviticus

SACRIFICES ARE COMPLETELY foreign to the twenty-first century. While we know the word and might even know of some religions with offerings labeled as sacrifices, actual blood sacrifices seem barbaric.

The first chapter of Leviticus opens with laws for the priests about how to kill a bull for a burnt offering. Leviticus can seem foreign to us. The feasts, the sacrifices, the festivals, and the laws about clean and unclean all can seem inapplicable to us. Therefore, reading Leviticus is daunting.

But every Christian should study Leviticus. The key ideas, introduced in chapter 1 and seen throughout the entire book, are holiness and atonement. How can Israel have a relationship with a holy God?

Exodus solidified God's selection of Israel as a nation to be His treasured possession. Through Israel came God's means of redemption for the entire world. But there is a problem. Israel was full of unredeemed people, obstinate people. While they quickly said they would follow God's covenant, they just as quickly turned aside to worship false gods, demonstrating themselves to be worse than the nations around them, as we will see in Judges.

Leviticus paves the way for us to understand God's holiness. Leviticus helps to answer the question of why God would kill Nadab and Abihu just for offering strange fire in the Tabernacle or why God would kill Uzzah for trying to steady the ark of the covenant when it was about to fall. If we shy away from Leviticus, we miss a great deal about the character of God.

Structure

When we first read through Leviticus, it can be difficult to see the structure and organization of the book. However, there is a clear division in Leviticus between chapters 16 and 17. Chapters 1–16 deal with the sacrificial system, the priesthood, laws about clean and unclean, and the Day of Atonement.

All these aspects have to do with how Israelites were to maintain their relationship with God.

Chapters 17–27 speak to the holy conduct of the people, the priests, the calendar, and the feasts. These chapters focus on how Israel was to reflect holiness in their daily activities.

Leviticus 1–16	The means of access to Yahweh
Leviticus 17–27	The walk of holiness in daily life

In addition to this major division, we can also see subdivisions in the book. The first seven chapters focus on the sacrificial system. Chapters 8–10 expound on the priesthood, its rules and function. Chapters 11–15 emphasize the distinction between what is clean and what is unclean, a theme that will be explained further later. Chapter 16 is certainly the heart of the book, speaking about the Day of Atonement, the most important day of the year for Israel. Chapter 17 focuses on restrictions to improper sacrifices, specifically mentioning the "goat idols." Chapters 18–20 command the holy conduct of the Israelites and chapters 21–22, the holy conduct of the priests. Chapters 23–25 deal with the holy times, the feasts and festivals. Chapter 26 is a pivotal chapter in the book, which will be examined in its own section. It includes blessings and curses for Israel. Finally, chapter 27 speaks to vows and tithing.

Purpose

The purpose of Leviticus can be summed up in a single word: holiness. The book of Leviticus, along with Isaiah, emphasizes the holiness of God—the fact that He is completely separate and distinct from humanity. This creator/creature distinction has its foundation in Genesis. Leviticus emphasizes this theme in every chapter. The issue that arises with the entry of sin into the world is the question of how can unholy people have a relationship with a holy God. This manifests itself in many ways in Leviticus, including with the story of Nadab and Abihu in Leviticus 10. This will also be seen in Numbers with the "plague" that breaks out against those who rebelled against God. But Leviticus sets the stage for a theology of the holy. To sum up the purpose of Leviticus in one sentence:

> **Leviticus purpose statement:** Holy Yahweh gives instruction to Israel concerning their holiness so that they might have fellowship with Yahweh.

Themes

While this is not meant to be an exhaustive list, the major themes of the book of Leviticus include the idea of holiness, the sacrifices, atonement, the priesthood, the Israelite calendar, and the feasts. Understanding how all of these themes fit together will give a comprehensive perspective on Leviticus.

Holiness

Holiness should be understood on a few different levels in Leviticus. Physical objects can be holy. The incense formula for the Tabernacle, outlined in Exodus 30, was considered holy (Exod. 30:37). The sacrifices in Leviticus 1–7 are described as holy. Even specials days (Sabbaths) and years (Year of Jubilee) were considered to be holy (Lev. 25:12). The priests were to be holy (21:8). All of these—whether things, people, animals, or times—were set apart. They had a purpose apart from their common, ordinary intent. These were all "set apart." When speaking about days, years, animals, food, items, and people, this had a causative sense. Someone set these apart to have a use outside of their common usage.

However, no one sets God apart as holy. God is Himself holy. For the created world, whether physical things or people, being holy has a starting place. Before the installation of Aaron and his sons as priests, they were not any more holy than any of the other Israelites. But God set them apart for a particular function, and they were to be regarded by all of Israel as being set apart.

Holiness for the created order means being "set apart." Holiness for God only means that He is "apart." God is in His nature completely distinct from His creation. A great example of this is the face of Moses when he came down from Mount Sinai. Exodus 34:29–35 recounts the story of Moses descending from Mount Sinai after speaking with the Lord. Moses' face shone brightly because he had been in the presence of the holy God.

Notice the reaction to God's holiness. The Israelites who saw Moses' face shining were terrified. We often do not think of God as terrifying and majestic, but this is an important characteristic of God. He causes terror to those who are not holy. The presence of God demands purity. Those who approach God in an unworthy manner face death.

Leviticus is almost entirely comprised of laws and regulations. However, Leviticus 10 is a narrative. This true story is meant to illustrate for the reader that what is unholy or profane cannot reside in the presence of God.

Nadab and Abihu were two of Aaron's sons. Aaron, Moses' brother, was the head of the priestly line. He had four sons, all of whom were set apart as priests. After God laid out the rules and regulations for the Tabernacle, Leviticus 10:1 says that Nadab and Abihu offered "strange fire" in their incense censers before the Lord. Yahweh's response was to send out fire from His presence to consume both Nadab and Abihu. The only explanation God gave was, "By those who come near Me, I will be treated as holy, and before all the people I will be honored" (Lev. 10:3).

Many hypotheses discuss what this strange fire was. The text does not make clear what was strange about the fire. What is important to notice from this text is that Nadab and Abihu knew they were doing something that was unauthorized. They knew they were acting against the ordinances of God. They were cutting corners and trying to do things their own way, which God's perfection would not tolerate.

At first glance, the story of Nadab and Abihu seems harsh. Unfortunately, that is because we do not treat God's holiness with the weight that we should. There is no compromise with God's holiness and perfection. He is separate from us.

For all of humanity's existence, being human has meant making mistakes, breaking God's laws. At no time in the existence of God has He made any mistakes. We are comforted to know that God does not change and never accepts second best. But this is also terrifying because God's nature cannot abide with our sinfulness. God says in Leviticus 19:2, "You shall be holy, for I, [Yahweh] your God, am holy."

Not only is God perfectly holy, but He expects His people to be holy as He is. For this very reason, the substitutionary atonement of Jesus Christ is the only way of salvation. All human fragility ends in one of two ways: either clothed in the perfection of Jesus based on faith in Jesus Christ or as Nadab and Abihu experienced, being consumed by the fiery wrath of God.

Sacrifices and Atonement

When speaking about sacrifices and atonement we must first understand blood. There is a "theology of blood" that goes back to Genesis. We see glimpses of it in the story of Cain and Abel. God said to Cain that his brother's blood was crying out to Him from the ground (Gen. 4:10).

Genesis 9:6 set down a law for capital punishment for anyone who "sheds man's blood." Even the phrase "your own flesh and blood" points to how the Hebrews understood blood.[1] The Passover demanded that the blood of a lamb be sprinkled on the doorposts so Yahweh would cause His judgment to pass over the house.

Blood represents life. Not all sacrifices require a blood offering. Five different types of sacrifices are laid out in Leviticus 1–7. The first offering that is described is the burnt offering. Only male animals were allowed for the burnt offering, though the type of animal would change depending on the economic status of the individual. A poor person would offer a male dove or pigeon. A ram or a bull would also be offered for the burnt offering, again depending on the economic ability of the individual. This offering was "to make atonement on his behalf" (Lev. 1:4).

The person who was making the offering would have to kill the animal himself, and the priests would sprinkle the blood around the altar. The carcass was then cut apart with the most of it being burned on top of the altar throughout the night, its ashes spread by the priest outside of the camp in the morning. The blood that is spilled out shows the price to be paid for sin.

One reason for sacrifices is to show the sinner the result of his sin. The bull or ram or dove was meant to be the sinner. Only by grace could the sinner have a substitute on his behalf. The sinner himself must actually do the deed of killing the animal to reinforce this understanding.

The second sacrifice was a grain offering, which was voluntary and demonstrated thankfulness for the firstfruits that God gave. It was always with unleavened bread, grain, or flour, which was mixed with olive oil and salt.

The third sacrifice, outlined in Leviticus 3, was the peace offering, also called the fellowship offering. This was for someone who wanted to make a vow or even show gratitude to God. Ultimately, this offering symbolized the fellowship that the person desired to have with God. Blood was also incorporated into this sacrifice, pointing to the requirement of life in order to have fellowship with God.

The fourth sacrifice, seen in Leviticus 4:1–5:13, was the sin offering. While the burnt offering was made for an intentional sin, the sin offering was made by someone who had sinned unintentionally or who needed to be cleansed. It did require the blood of an animal, unless the person making the offering was extremely poor, in which case it could be an offering of flour.

The fifth sacrifice, seen in Leviticus 5:14–6:7 and 7:1–6, was the guilt offering. This was made by someone who had deprived another person

---

1 See for example, Genesis 15:4 (NIV), where God promised a son to Abraham who was to be Abraham's own "flesh and blood."

of his rights or had desecrated something holy. This offering required a ram or a lamb without blemish for the offering, regardless of the person's socioeconomic status.

All of these sacrifices and offerings were to be made in the Tabernacle complex. If the commands were followed, then the number of sacrifices made each day would be staggering. Imagine needing to make a sacrifice every time you sinned or acted wrongly against another person.

The most important sacrifice was made on the Day of Atonement. Leviticus 16 is dedicated to this. The Day of Atonement was a yearly ceremony in which the high priest was required to cleanse himself and his clothes, make a sacrifice of a bull and two goats, and sprinkle the blood of the bull on the mercy seat of the ark of the covenant inside the Holy of Holies in order to make atonement for the entire nation of Israel. With one of the goats, the high priest is to do the same as with the bull, placing the blood on the mercy seat. In addition, the blood of the bull and of the goat was placed on the altar to cleanse the altar for another year of service. This was because the Tabernacle "abides with them in the midst of their impurities" (Lev. 16:16).

A final note to make on sacrifices is the extent of their atoning power. Did the sacrifices actually make atonement for the sins of the people or were they just representative? The book of Hebrews is of great help here. Hebrews 10:4 says, "For it is impossible for the blood of bulls and goats to take away sins." The author of Hebrews is contrasting the sacrifice of Christ, once for all, which makes complete atonement for His people. To help answer this question concerning what Old Testament sacrifices accomplished, we must first examine the idea of the clean and the unclean.

Clean and Unclean

We have already introduced the separation between what is holy and what is common. In addition to this, there is the concept of the separation between the clean and the unclean. This distinction is even seen as early as Genesis 7 with the flood, where God commanded Noah to take seven pairs of every clean animal and only one pair of every unclean animal with him into the ark. The distinction between clean and unclean existed before the flood, but it is not seen in the creation. No mention is made of God calling some animals unclean when He created them. The distinction between clean and unclean has to do with the effects of sin in the world.[2] This contrasts with

2 We might even point to the subjection of the creation by God after the fall. Romans 8:20 says the creation was subjected to futility by God.

sin, which is an act of rebellion against God. And one can also point to evil, which is the heart impetus for doing sinful actions.

Therefore, the evil of the human heart brings about the breaking of God's laws (sin and transgression), which is manifest in the results of sin being in the world (clean and unclean). The unclean includes certain animals, such as any kind of water animal that does not have scales and fins; several types of birds, including the vulture, the raven, and the bat; and several species of crawling animals, such as mice, lizards, and geckos. Also, any carcass of an animal that has died of old age or has not been killed for meat is considered unclean.

People who have certain diseases are unclean including lepers. Also, a woman who has just given birth is considered unclean. This can be shocking to us. After all, what is wrong with giving birth? But we must remember that being unclean doesn't imply guilt. The distinction between clean and unclean has to do with the effects of sin in the world.

One effect of sin being in the world is death. Before sin entered the world, there was no death. Now that sin is in the world, death reigns over all living things, except for Christ.

So, one manifestation of sin being in the world is death. Another would be the fact that there are diseases. A person who has a disease is not any more sinful that someone who does not.[3] The distinction between clean and unclean has to do with the general manifestation of the effects of sin in the world. The example of a woman giving birth also highlights this point. The woman was the one who brought life into the world. That newness of life is beautiful and wonderful. But all children who are born into the world will sin. The act of giving life to another human baby means that sin will continue to be perpetuated.

Because of this, a woman who gave birth to a boy is unclean for forty days. However, a woman who gives birth to a girl is unclean for eighty days because not only is she bringing a human life into the world, but that baby will one day, Lord willing, bring another life into the world as well (Lev. 12:1–5). Laws of purification included making sacrifices, bathing in water, and other ritual cleansing.

---

3 An excellent example of this is the story of the man born blind in John 9. The disciples asked Jesus what sin caused the man to be blind, since he was that way from birth. Jesus answered that the man's condition had nothing to do with him committing a specific sin that he was being punished for. We might also point to the story of Job and the false accusations his friends made, saying he suffered because he had some secret sin in his life.

The Calendar

Before finishing our overview of Leviticus, let's examine both the calendar and the feasts of Israel. As mentioned previously, particular days and years were holy. The Sabbath was one that was well-known. Every seventh day was a day of rest. The Israelites were required to take that day of rest seriously. In fact, the Sabbath was the sign of the Mosaic covenant, which will be fully examined when we discuss the book of Numbers.

There was also the Sabbath year. One year in seven was meant to be a year of rest for the land. For six years, the people sowed their fields and harvested their vineyards. On the seventh, they were not allowed to sow seed or prune their vineyards. The Lord promised that He would provide an abundance in the sixth year, which would supply His people until the start of the next cycle of years. This is outlined in Leviticus 25:1–7.

It is interesting to note that when the people of Israel were deported to Babylon, many centuries from the time of the writing of Leviticus, part of the reason they were deported was because they were not observing the Sabbath years. Second Chronicles 36:21 says that God allowed the land to enjoy its Sabbath years because the Israelites, in their greed, had not observed the Sabbath years. Israel neglected seventy years' worth of Sabbath years, which is the amount of time they were in exile. This is even prophesied in Leviticus 26:34–35, where God said that if Israel did not keep the covenant, He would deport them to give the land its Sabbath rest.

Besides the Sabbath years, Israel was required to observe the Year of Jubilee, outlined in Leviticus 25:8–22. The fiftieth year was the Year of Jubilee, after seven sets of seven years. The Jubilee was a very special year when all land reverted back to the family God had given it to, and all Israelite slaves were set free.

In the book of Joshua, we see that God apportioned the land of Canaan out by tribe, clan, and family. If a family had a financial crisis and had to sell their land, they would receive it back in the Jubilee year. For this reason, someone purchasing the land paid a price based only on the amount of return that he or she would receive from the land until the Year of Jubilee. If Jubilee was the next year, then the price for the land would be one-fiftieth of what it would be the year right after Jubilee.

In the same way, if an Israelite had to sell himself into slavery to pay for his debts, he would work only until the Jubilee and then be set free. Depending on when the next Jubilee was, prices and transactions were adjusted accordingly.

In this way, indentured servitude was not permanent, and no family ever lost their land inheritance from the Lord. Also, the people were not allowed to sow or cultivate the land. On the forty-eighth year, Yahweh would provide enough for them to sustain themselves on the forty-ninth year, which was a Sabbath year, and in the fiftieth year, the Year of Jubilee.

The Feasts

Leviticus 23 outlines the feasts that were to be holy throughout the year. The Sabbath day was considered a feast day. The Passover, already briefly mentioned, was to be celebrated on the fourteenth day of the first month of Israel's calendar. The start of the day was actually at twilight. For example, the Sabbath would start on our Friday at twilight and end on our Saturday at twilight. In this way, the Passover began on the night of the fourteenth day of the first month, with the Feast of Unleavened Bread being on the fifteenth. The Passover was a solemn feast, reminding the Israelites of their deliverance through the death that surrounded them in Egypt.

The Feast of Firstfruits varied from year to year because the festival was based on the first fruit that came from the harvest. Once the first fruit or grain appeared, it was to be cut off and waved before the Lord as a sign of thanks for His provision on the next Sabbath day. It was to be accompanied with a sacrifice of a year-old male lamb. From the time of the Feast of Firstfruits, a clock began ticking until the fiftieth day after Firstfruits, which was considered the Feast of Weeks. This is Pentecost, as seen in the book of Acts. The Israelite was to present a grain offering and a burnt offering to the Lord for the Feast of Weeks.

The Feast of Trumpets is on the first day of the seventh month. On it, a trumpets were blasted as a memorial, and the Israelites were to rest from any work. The Day of Atonement was ten days after the Feast of Trumpets. Finally, Leviticus outlines the Feast of Booths. This commemorated the wanderings of Israel in the wilderness. It was to start on the fifteenth day of the seventh month and go for seven days. Each family was to construct a and live in a booth for seven days, to remember the time they lived in the wilderness. As outlined in Leviticus, these feast days were to remind Israel that Yahweh was their God (Lev. 23:43).

Leviticus 26

A final note to make about Leviticus is the all-important chapter 26. This chapter recites for Israel the blessings and the curses. This is done again in

Deuteronomy 28 with the second giving of the Law. Taking into account all that is discussed about God's holiness and Israel's sin, chapter 26 is a terrifying climax to Leviticus.

As will be outlined in Deuteronomy, Israel did not have a heart that followed after God. They could not accomplish their promise that they would follow the commands, set out by God in Exodus 19:8, since their hearts were wicked. But nevertheless, God explained the consequences if they disobeyed and the blessings if they obeyed.

The blessings that are promised spoke to God's desire for Israel to follow Him. If they were true to the covenant and their relationship with Yahweh, Yahweh would send them rain at the right time; the fields and trees would yield their produce abundantly so that they would not be able to keep up with the harvesting; they would have no enemies or anyone to make them afraid; there would be no pestilence, marauders, or even wild beasts in their lands; God would dwell with them, walking among them, and they would be known as the people of Yahweh.

On the opposing side, if Israel disobeyed, they would be stricken with panic, wasting disease, and fever; they would show their seed in vain; their enemies would rule over them; their harvests would be empty; wild beasts would terrorize them and bereave them of children and livestock; their cities would be laid waste; their roads desolate.

The description of the judgment of God against Israel should they not keep the covenant was horrific. And all of these things came to pass in the rest of the Old Testament. Stories about the judgment of Yahweh on Israel are meant to point back to this chapter and to Deuteronomy 28. In a way, the history of Israel is foretold in this chapter.

Leviticus is often described as a difficult book to read. But time spent studying Leviticus is never wasted. Leviticus shows us the seriousness of God's holiness. It also paves the way for the theology of atonement. It emphasizes the problem of a holy God having relationship with an unholy people. Ultimately, it points us to Christ who is the One who makes a way for us to have relationship with a perfectly holy God.

Study questions:

1. Have you found Leviticus to be a challenging read in the past? If so, how has this chapter affected your desire to read Leviticus?
2. What does it mean for God to be holy? Would you say you have a high view of the holiness of God?
3. What does it mean for humans to be holy? How does this impact the way you read passages that describes believers as holy?
4. What is the significance of the Day of Atonement? How does this shed light on your understanding of the doctrine of atonement?
5. What is the relationship between the clean/unclean distinction and the notion of sin? Are the two synonymous?
6. What is the purpose of the book of Leviticus?

4

Numbers

NUMBERS IS A SEVERE book. If you have spent time reading through the book, you have probably wondered about the severity of God. Many examples of severity exist throughout the book. Numbers 15:32–36 contains a brief story about a man who went out to pick up sticks in order to build himself a fire to cook his food. The only problem was that he was picking up sticks on the Sabbath. The consequence was that he was stoned to death.

Numbers 11:31–35 is a story about how Israel told Yahweh that they were tired of eating manna. God sent them quail for meat. But as the people were greedily eating the meat, God sent a "very great plague" that killed many Israelites. Numbers 21:4–9 tells the story of Israel complaining again. The text says that Israel became impatient. Yahweh answered by sending fiery serpents among the people, which killed many. In this story we see the serpent on the pole, raised up above the people, so that any who looked on the bronze serpent were saved from death. This sign of the bronze serpent on a pole has been borrowed by the American Medical Association.

But in reading Numbers, we are introduced to a severe book, a harshness that we do not see in everyday life. Besides the severity, we also find unique stories, such as Balaam's talking donkey and the budding of Aaron's staff. All these stories point to the purpose of the book which is also reflected in the structure of the book.

Structure

The major structure of Numbers has to do with the different generations of Israel. Chapters 1–25 deal with the first generation—those Israelites who came up out of Egypt. Chapters 26–36 deal with the second generation—primarily those who were born while Israel wandered the wilderness.

The first generation was those who saw the wonders of God in Egypt and the miracles God did for them. They were at Mount Sinai when the Ten

Commandments were given. This first generation said a hearty "yes" to the Mosaic covenant, "All that Yahweh says we will do." However, as Israel wandered in the wilderness for forty years, a generational transition occurred.

The second generation also saw the glory of Yahweh. Yahweh was dwelling in the Tabernacle, and they could see His glory in the cloud by day and pillar of fire by night. The second generation, along with the first, experienced the blessing of Yahweh in His provision for them. They experienced picking up the manna from the ground each day. They saw how Yahweh provided water for them in the wilderness. But the key question is, "Who was the second generation?" Were they the same as the first generation or had they changed? This was the test case for Israel. How did they respond to Yahweh's faithfulness and provision? This changeover in generations shows us the true heart of Israel, not just a single generation.

Besides the major structure of Numbers, we can also see sub-structure. Within the first block, chapters 1–25, there is division between chapters 1–10, chapters 11–21, and chapters 22–25.

During the time frame of chapters 1–10, Israel was still at Mount Sinai. In Leviticus, the emphasis was on the commands and regulations that Israel received at Mount Sinai. The beginning of Numbers picks right back up where Leviticus left off. Chapters 1–10 explain the organization of Israel with the Tabernacle as the center of the camp.

Chapters 11–21 start off on a negative note. Chapter 11 tells about the journey from Sinai to Kadesh, and along the way, the people complained about God's provision. Even when the people arrived at Kadesh, they continued to complain and even openly rebel against Yahweh, as will be seen in chapters 13–20. After being at Kadesh, the people then set out to Moab and complained along the way again in chapter 21.

Chapters 22–25 show a key example of Israel and their unfaithfulness to Yahweh. This encompasses the story of Balak and Balaam, which we will further explore. However, the rebellion of Israel continued to fester and eventually led to idolatry and open wickedness. All of these stories emphasize the wickedness of the first generation, those who came up out of Egypt and saw the wonders and miracles that Yahweh performed for them in Egypt.

The second major section of Numbers deals with the second generation. The book of Numbers covers forty years of history, from the leaving of Mount Sinai, through the wilderness wanderings to Israel, and moving through Moab up to the point before the Israelites were about to cross the

Jordan River and go into Canaan. Chapters 26–36 deal with Israel on the plains of Moab, where they prepared to enter the land to conquer it.

Within these chapters is an attempt to renew the obedience of Israel. A new census takes place to determine how many Israelites there are (Num. 26). Joshua is identified as the successor to Moses (27:12–23). The offerings and feasts are recounted to remind the people that they are supposed to be set apart and holy to Yahweh (28–29). Chapter 31 is the story of the vengeance Israel takes on Midian, who led them into idolatry. The boundaries of the land of Canaan and the inheritance for each of the tribes was determined in chapter 34.

All of these things point to an attempt to renew obedience after all of the rebellion of the first generation. Ultimately, this separation from the first generation to the second is the basis for the structure of Numbers and tells us about the intention behind the writing of the book.

Purpose

Numbers tells a bleak story about Israel. The book has an intermingling of commands and narrative. As a contrast, Leviticus is primarily a book of commands. However, both the legal portions of Numbers and the narratives point to a central purpose of the book.

> **Numbers purpose statement:** Israel fails to obey Yahweh which leads to judgment and death; however, this does not ultimately frustrate Yahweh's purpose to bless Israel.

We see death occur repeatedly in Numbers. Israel would rebel and God would send a plague. Israel then would repent and turn back to God, but ultimately continued to grumble and complain against God. This cycle occurred again and again.

The first generation, even though they saw the power and provision of God, did not follow after God with their whole heart. The cycle began again with the second generation, leaving the question at the end of the book of whether the second generation would indeed obey and love Yahweh.

Themes

Many themes fill the book of Numbers. Perhaps the most prominent is the rebellion and grumbling of Israel and how that affected Israel's entrance into the Promised Land. But the blessing of Yahweh is also seen throughout Numbers, despite Israel's rebellion.

Certainly, a central theme of Numbers is the counting of the people and the emphasis on the tribe of Levi.

The Promised Land and the Grumbling of Israel

The story from Numbers that is most often told in Sunday School is that of the twelve spies sent into the land of Canaan. This was a pivotal point in the history of Israel and especially in the book of Numbers.

Even though this was a pivotal point, the history of Israel before this point showed a pattern of rebellion against Yahweh. The fact that Israel took Egyptian idols with them out of Egypt and through the parted Red Sea points to their rebellion from the start. They rebelled with the golden calf even though they could see the manifestation of Yahweh on Mount Sinai. They thought they needed to create a physical idol even though they could see the presence of Yahweh and see the cloud and fire.

They also grumbled from Mount Sinai to the border of Canaan. Numbers 11 and 12 outline their grumbling from the lowest of them all the way up the ranks to Moses' brother, Aaron, and his sister, Miriam. It is not surprising, then, when we arrive at the story of the twelve spies to see that Israel rebelled again.

One man was chosen from each tribe and these men were sent into the Promised Land for forty days. They returned with amazing stories of the produce and beauty of the land, but also with stories of the strong-walled cities, fierce people, and even giants that lived in the land.

Israel, having experienced God bringing Egypt, the most powerful nation on the earth at that time, to its knees, did not believe they could defeat the Canaanites. Only two of the spies, Caleb and Joshua, heartily approved invading the land, knowing that Yahweh was on their side.

The people did not listen to Joshua and Caleb, and so God punished them by banishing them to the wilderness until the first generation of those who left Egypt died in the wilderness. They wandered in the wilderness for forty years, one year for every day the spies were in the land. Additionally, Numbers 14:37 says God struck down with a plague the ten spies who brought the bad report.

Again and again, the cycle of rebellion, judgment, and mercy is seen in Numbers. Even in the case of the people's rebellion at the border of Canaan, God did not wipe the people out. He had mercy on those who were not of decision-making age, the second generation. God maintained His commitment to the promises made to Abraham, Isaac, and Jacob. The story of the bronze serpent is another key example of God's mercy after the rebellion and judgment of Israel.

Numbers 21:4–9 recounts another episode of Israel's rebellion. In this case, they became impatient and spoke against Yahweh and Moses. We must remember that this grumbling was about the comprehensive provision that God had given the people. They had all their food and water provided each day. They had defeated all of those who attacked them. They had the presence of Yahweh before their eyes. And yet they continued to grumble.

For this reason, Yahweh sent fiery serpents among them, and they appealed for mercy. The mercy Yahweh sent them was in the form of a bronze serpent on a pole. If anyone who was bitten by a serpent looked at the bronze serpent, they would be spared. Second Kings 18:4 even mentions that Israel kept the bronze serpent after this point and worshipped it as an idol. Rather than worshipping Yahweh the Creator, they chose again and again to worship the creature, the image, the idol.

The Blessing of Yahweh

In thinking about the theme of the blessing of Yahweh in Numbers, we must keep in mind Leviticus 26. Israel was committed to the Mosaic covenant, and Yahweh promised that if they were faithful to the covenant, then He would bless them more than they could imagine. But if they disobeyed, Yahweh would bring awful curses upon them.

Even though they quickly accepted these terms, their hearts continually lead them astray. God certainly punished their sin, but even though they continually disobeyed, God did not bring all these curses upon them. Rather, Yahweh blessed them even when they did not deserve it.

The first example of this is the giving of the land of Canaan. Israel had not demonstrated holiness, but God still promised them Canaan—a land of great bounty and beauty. Even when the people rebelled at the border, God still promised the land to the second generation. God gave the land to the national of Israel, but it was also a blessing for every family. Each family was allotted a particular portion of the land, which would never be taken from them. Even if they sold their portion of the land, it would revert back to them in the Year of Jubilee.

A question arises in Numbers 27 about a man named Zelophehad in the first generation, who would die in the wilderness, but who only had daughters. When his daughters were married off to other families, what would happen to his allotted land?

Moses asked the Lord this, and Yahweh responded by saying that the land gift was valid for the daughters of Zelophehad as well. They were entitled to keep the land that was promised to them, even though they had married into other families. This demonstrates the faithfulness of God in keeping his promises, even down to the individual families of Israel.

Another key example of God's faithfulness and blessing is the story of Balaam and Balak, the well-known story that included a talking donkey. This story took place right after Israel defeated Sihon, king of the Amorites and Og, king of Bashan. The next king to face on the march to the border of Canaan was Balak, king of the Moabites. Balak was afraid because there were so many more Israelites than men in his army, so he called upon Balaam, a prophet, to come and curse the people of Israel. Balaam was called a prophet, but he was no prophet of Yahweh.

In ancient times, prophets existed in many places. We see the magicians and prophets of Egypt, who were at odds against Moses. They even had some power; they were not just snake-oil salesmen. Balaam was a well-known prophet who was located several hundred miles from Balak. Balaam lived near the Euphrates River. His reputation was as a hirable prophet who, for the right price, would do what you needed. Balak saw Balaam as his way out of this conflict with Israel.

Yahweh even spoke to Balaam and told him to go with Balak's men. However, on the way, because of Balaam's greed, Yahweh placed the angel of the Lord in front of Balaam to kill him. In an unexpected twist, Balaam's donkey, afraid for its life, wouldn't proceed. Balaam, unaware of the danger he was in, beat the donkey.

God opened the donkey's mouth to tell Balaam about the danger he was in. God then relented and allowed Balaam to arrive in Moab. Balaam, hoping to follow the wishes of Balak, went out to Israel. But instead of cursing Israel, God used Balaam to bless Israel three times. From Revelation 2:14, we learn that Balaam then gave Balak the idea to seduce the people of Israel into idolatry and sexual immorality.

How did Israel respond to Yahweh's protection and blessing of them in the Balak and Balaam narrative? They turned to the idols of Moab, worshipped Baal of Peor, and fell into sexual sin with Moabite women.

In response, in Numbers 25, God sent a devastating plague against Israel, which ultimately killed 24,000 Israelites. It stopped only because of the righteous zeal of Phinehas, a priest in the line of Aaron. When Phinehas saw an Israelite blatantly taking a Moabite woman into his tent, Phinehas rose up and killed them both with a spear, and thus, the plague was lifted. Because of Phinehas' righteous zeal, Yahweh made a covenant of priesthood with him and his descendants.

The Tribes of Israel and the Priestly Line

The book of Numbers is appropriately named in our English Bibles. There is a major emphasis on the organization of the tribes of Israel, their numerical growth, and the divisions of responsibilities.

While Israel was in Egypt, we see no indication that any of the tribes saw themselves as the head of Israel. Certainly, Jacob's blessing of his children in Genesis 49 pointed to Judah as an important tribe within Israel. And Leviticus emphasized the role of the tribe of Levi. Numbers pointed to the organization of all of the tribes, and this can be seen in the layout of the camp.

The Tabernacle was always to sit in the center of the Israelite camp. The placement of the tribes of Israel around the Tabernacle was important. The primary place was the eastern side of the Tabernacle. Judah held this prominent position with Issachar and Zebulun on Judah's right and left sides respectively. Reuben, the firstborn, occupied the center of the south side with Simeon and Gad to the west and east of Reuben. Ephraim stood at the center of the western side with Manasseh and Benjamin to the north and south. Finally, Dan stood at the center of the northern side with Asher and Naphtali to the west and east. Judah held the most prominent position, and Reuben, Manasseh, and Dan also had leadership roles within Israel.

We can also see this layout based on prominence with the Levites. The Levites were divided into several different clans. Levi had three sons: Gershon, Kohath, and Merari. These three made up the clans of Levi. From the Kohath clan came Aaron, who was the head of the Aaronic priesthood line. The clan of Gershon camped at the west of the Tabernacle, Merari to the north, and Kohath to the south. However, Aaron and his sons, as well as Moses, placed their tents in front of Judah, on the eastern side between the Tabernacle and Judah.

This again shows the prominence of the Aaronic line. Although Aaron was from the clan of Kohath, God chose him to be the head of the priestly line. In this way, all Levities were to be servants in the Tabernacle, each clan with its own responsibilities, but only Aaron's descendants could be priests.

In the study of Exodus, we noticed that the price God required of Israel when He took them out of Egypt was their firstborn. God spared the firstborn of Israel and killed the firstborn of the Egyptians. This was not because Israel was holier or had done anything to earn God's favor. While the Egyptian firstborn died, God spared the firstborn of Israel and delivered all of Israel out of Egypt. Therefore, the firstborn of Israel belonged to Yahweh, dedicated to Yahweh for service.

Numbers 3:40–51 explains how the firstborns of every tribe of Israel were replaced with the entire tribe of Levi. The counting of Israel showed that 22,273 firstborns were in Israel. This was 273 more than the total number of Levites. Therefore, God had Israel pay five shekels for each of these excess firstborns to Aaron and his sons. In this way, all of the firstborns of Israel were ransomed by the tribe of Levi, which was now wholly dedicated to the service of Yahweh.

The Levites had particular responsibilities depending on their clan. The Kohathites ministered over the holy things. They were in charge of the transportation, upkeep, and guarding of all the holy things of the Tabernacle. In Numbers 4, we also see that the Gershonites were given responsibilities of serving and carrying portions of the Tabernacle. The Merarites were given the task of carrying the remaining portions of the Tabernacle whenever the camp of Israel moved.

Each of the Levites worked in the service of the Tabernacle from the ages of thirty to fifty. According to Numbers 8:24, the Levites began their training at age twenty-five. Additionally, after the age of fifty they were allowed to keep guard, but they could not serve in other ways. The Levites received their income from the payment of tithe and food from the sacrifices. Therefore, the Levites were taken care of their entire lives, including enjoying a retirement after fifty years of age, through the Tabernacle ministry. This was their inheritance because they were not allotted land as the other tribes had.

While the Levites did not receive any land as an inheritance, God did give them several cities within Canaan. Numbers 35 lists the cities they received. This included 1500 feet in all directions around the city for pastureland for the Levites' animals. These cities were spread throughout Israel so the Levites would minister to all the tribes of Israel. The Levites' most important responsibilities were to the Tabernacle, its protection, maintenance, and transportation. However, the Levites were also meant to be spiritual fathers to Israel.

One unique aspect of the cities of the Levites is that some of the cities were chosen to be cities of refuge. Numbers 35:9–34 identifies six of these cities, evenly spread out over the "soon-to-be" territory of Israel. Genesis 9:6 stipulates that anyone who shed man's blood, by man his blood would be shed. However, the question arose about what to do with an accidental death. Israel had no police department. Instead, if someone was killed, that person's closest male relative who was of age would act as the avenger against the murderer (Num. 35:19). But if the murderer was not truly a murderer, and the death was accidental, the one who killed was permitted to flee to a Levitical city of refuge, where the family avenger could not enter to take vengeance.

Numbers 35:12 also points to a "congregation" that was able to put the supposed murderer on trial. The city of refuge was a place of safety until a verdict could be established. These cities were evenly spread through the land so people could reach them in only a few days from anywhere in Israel.

Study Questions:

1. Would you describe God as a severe God? How does this view of God reconcile with God's loving nature?
2. Why might God have been severe in the book of Numbers?
3. What is the purpose of the book of Numbers?
4. How is the purpose of the book of Numbers reflected in the structure?
5. What do you learn from the story of the snakes and the bronze serpent?
6. What do you learn from the fact that Israel turned the bronze serpent into an idol?

5

Deuteronomy

DEUTERONOMY IS A theological book. Certainly, all books in the Bible are theological in nature, but the main point of Deuteronomy has to do with understanding who God is. The organization of Deuteronomy is based around this. Moses spoke directly to the people for almost all of Deuteronomy, trying to help them understand who God is and their place before Yahweh. Deuteronomy, like Genesis or Isaiah, is one of those pinnacle books of the Old Testament. It deserves attention and careful study.

Structure

Deuteronomy has a clear structure. It is based around the speeches (or one might say the sermons) of Moses. Moses gives three sermons in Deuteronomy followed up by the Song of Moses and the Blessing of Moses.

Deuteronomy 1:1–4:43	The First Sermon of Moses
Deuteronomy 4:44–28:68	The Second Sermon of Moses
Deuteronomy 29:1–30:20	The Third Sermon of Moses
Deuteronomy 31:1–32:47	The Song of Moses
Deuteronomy 32:48–34:12	The Blessing of Moses

The first sermon of Moses highlighted the history of Israel from the point of leaving Mount Sinai until their interaction with Moab. Moses wanted Israel, from the beginning of his sermons, to understand where they came from. He wanted to remind them of how God sustained them, but he also reminded them of their pattern of rebelling against God.

Repeated throughout the section was the idea that God is holy and all-powerful. As Deuteronomy 3:24 states, "O [Yahweh] God, You have begun to show Your servant Your greatness and Your strong hand; for what god is there in heaven or on earth who can do such works and mighty acts as Yours?" This first sermon ended with an exhortation to obey the Law of God in Deuteronomy 4:1–40. Moses pointed to the uniqueness of Israel's situation. They alone had the laws of God (Deut. 4:8). No other nation, no matter how strong and mighty, had the ordinances of God.

In addition, what other nation had a god who dwelled with them? Only Yahweh dwells with His people (4:7). Yahweh has also made His covenant with Israel.

All of these truths should have challenged the people to wholeheartedly follow God. Even Paul points to this in Romans 9:4–5 when he said that to Israel belonged the adoption, the glory, the covenants, the giving of the Law, the worship, the promises, and the patriarchs.

Moses pulled on the same argument and stresses to Israel that they were greatly blessed above all other nations, and so they should devote themselves completely to Yahweh.

Moses' second sermon was the longest in Deuteronomy and reiterated the Mosaic covenant and the Law. The Ten Commandments were given again in Deuteronomy 5:1–21. This forms the basis for the entire Law.

Deuteronomy 6:4–5 is the "Shema" of Israel, which we will discuss in more detail. The Shema pointed to the heart of the Law and gave the simple command that Israel was to love Yahweh their God.

Chapters 5–11 gave more reasons why Israel should have obeyed the Law. And chapters 12–26 spoke to specific stipulations for Israel keeping the Law in the Promised Land. Chapters 27 and 28 reemphasize Leviticus 26 and the blessings and curses. Moses gave Israel every reason to obey the Law and to love Yahweh.

The third sermon of Moses was the actual making of another covenant with Israel. There is a debate as to whether this is a renewal of the Mosaic covenant or a new covenant altogether. This third sermon is in chapters 29–30. While there is some debate as to this covenant's nature, Deuteronomy 29:1 makes it clear that this covenant is "besides the covenant which He had made with them at Horeb [Mount Sinai]." The Israelites broke the Mount Sinai covenant again and again. This renewal, or making of a new covenant, in Deuteronomy 29–30, ensured another chance for Israel to follow Yahweh with their whole heart.

The last two sections of Deuteronomy were the Song of Moses (31:1–32:47) and the Blessing of Moses (32:48–34:12). Moses was about to die, and Israel recognized this as a pivotal time in their history.

Moses was the first leader of Israel and acted as an intermediary between Israel and God. Moses again and again appealed to God to not destroy Israel, and God listened to Moses' appeals.

Now that Moses was about to die, and Joshua would take over as ruler, it was important for Moses to tell the people what they needed to do and what would happen to them.

This same intention was seen with the death of Jacob at the end of Genesis. In Genesis 49, Jacob gathered all of his sons and told them what would happen to them in the coming days (Gen. 49:1). Moses was doing something similar in Deuteronomy 31–34. Moses' blessing in chapter 33 was even directed to each of the individual tribes.

It is interesting to note that Moses did not bless the tribes in order of largest to smallest or of oldest to youngest. Reuben, who was the firstborn, was first, but Judah, the fourth born, was next.

Each blessing of the tribes was different. For example, Moses blessed Reuben by simply saying, "May Reuben live and not die; / Nor his men be few" (Deut. 33:6). No mention was made of a promised Messiah from Judah. Levi was emphasized as the spiritual leader. Moses asked that Joseph (both Manasseh and Ephraim) be blessed with the choice things of heaven. Moses said that Joseph's tribe was "distinguished among his brothers" (33:16). Each tribe was given a unique blessing.

While most of Deuteronomy is comprised of law and command, Deuteronomy 34, the last chapter, is narrative, telling the story of Moses' death. According to this chapter, God took Moses to the top of Mount Nebo, opposite the Promised Land, and showed Moses all the land.

Moses died there, and the text says that God buried Moses "in the valley in the land of Moab, opposite Beth-peor; but no man knows his burial place to this day" (34:6).

The Israelites mourned for Moses for thirty days, and then Joshua took command of the people of Israel. The Pentateuch ends with this description of Moses in Deuteronomy 34:10–12:

> Since that time no prophet has risen in Israel like Moses, whom [Yahweh] knew face to face, for all the signs and wonders which [Yahweh] sent him to perform in the land of Egypt against Pharaoh, all his servants, and all his land, and for all the mighty power and for all the great terror which Moses performed in the sight of all Israel.

Purpose

The purpose of Deuteronomy can be seen in its structure and the themes that run deeply throughout the book. Deuteronomy is sermonic in nature, and it has a clear purpose.

> **Deuteronomy purpose statement:** Moses exhorts Israel to fear Yahweh, keep His commands, and be faithful to the covenant even though Israel does not have a heart to obey Yahweh.

At the heart of the book is the need for Israel to fear and love Yahweh. These two were not mutually exclusive in this book; but they had an important relationship, as we will discover. The issue Moses pointed out several times in the book was that Israel did not have a heart that would follow Yahweh. They continued to rebel against Him.

Themes

Deuteronomy, as a pinnacle book of the Old Testament, has themes that are seen in many other books. Besides the Psalter, the New Testament quotes Deuteronomy more than any other Old Testament book because these themes are essential to understanding who God is and what God has done for us. Themes of Deuteronomy include love for God, the law and principle, the fear of God, and the heart of a Yahweh follower.

Love for God: The Shema

The Shema is at the heart of Deuteronomy. Deuteronomy 6:4–5 says, "Hear, O Israel! [Yahweh] is our God, [Yahweh] is one! You shall love [Yahweh] your God with all your heart and with all your soul and with all your might."

This encompasses what Deuteronomy is all about. First was the command for Israel to pay attention because what was coming was important. In addition, God was described as One. This is a simple statement, but the ramifications of this statement are vast. God as one is self-contained, needing nothing, with no beginning and no end. Deuteronomy elaborates on the character of Yahweh throughout the book.

The command that arises out of God being one is that Israel was to love. The obedience was spoken of after this point, but love was the first command. Love and obedience are linked throughout the book. The issue was that Israel did not have a heart that loved God. Their obedience was contingent on outward blessing. When things were going well, they forgot

God. When things were not going well, they grumbled against God. The qualification for the command was that it was love with all the heart, soul, and might. Nothing would be held back from loving God, no matter what the circumstances. At this point in their history, Israel had failed to connect their inward devotion to their outward actions. Their inward devotion changed, so their outward adherence to the Law was faulty. They misunderstood the connection between law and principle.

Law and Principle

Many Christians ask what relevance the Old Testament Law has to the Christian today. Certainly, we see God at work in the Pentateuch, and we can see His character. God was faithful to work with Israel, keeping His promises and showing His loving-kindness to Israel.

We also see God as all-powerful, the One who created everything and has authority over everything. And we recognize that the church of today is not the Israel of the Old Testament. Therefore, how does the church-going Christian relate to the laws of Israel?

To this point in studying the Pentateuch, we have encountered a lot of different types of laws. Some laws don't make sense to us immediately. Wearing clothing not woven of two types of material or building a parapet around your roof seems foreign to us.

We can initially see some of the reasoning behind the laws. For example, the parapet law we initially understand was based on needing to take care of those visiting our homes, that they do not have an accident and fall off the roof. But there are also laws for sacrifices, not just laws concerning daily life and work. For example, why the law about the fat of each sacrifice belonging to the Lord?

However, we also see some laws that are much greater in scope. Deuteronomy 6:5 is a law: Love Yahweh. It is a command in the same sense as building a parapet is a command. But the parapet is much more closely tied to physical action. Either you have a parapet, or you do not. But loving God is up for debate as to how to implement that law. It is not a law that can just be crossed off the list like the parapet law.

This is the debate that Jesus had with the Pharisees. The Pharisees imagined they could just check off all of the laws of the Old Testament and be right with God. If they needed to tithe, they made sure everything they owned was tithed, including anything small like the herbs that they grew. They mistakenly thought that the law of God was something they could check off on a list and earn their favor with God. But they missed the heart of the Law, and we must be careful not to do the same.

Jesus, in Matthew 5–7, pointed to the heart of lawgiving. The Pharisees assumed that they had kept the sixth commandment if they had not killed anyone. But Jesus said that if you are angry with your brother, you have violated the same Law. Likewise, the seventh commandment to not commit adultery can be broken by lusting, even though no action is taken. Jesus pointed to the intention of the Law. Paul explained that the Law brings wrath.

The intention of the Law was to point out sin. The Law itself is perfect. However, as Paul pointed out in Romans 7:7–8, "Is the Law sin? May it never be! On the contrary, I would not have come to know sin except through the Law; for I would not have known about coveting if the Law had not said, 'You shall not covet.' But sin, taking opportunity through the commandment, produced in me coveting of every kind."

This is the picture that is painted for us in the Pentateuch. The perfect Law, given to Israel at a particular time, pointed out Israel's wickedness. The Law was a measuring stick that showed Israel their faults and the wickedness of their corrupted hearts.

Each law is based on a principle that points the adherent back to God. We can think of the Law as the outworking of a principle that is rooted in the character of God. God, being a God of love, sheds light on the principle of loving God and loving your neighbor, which is then manifested in thousands of different laws at different times.

God is holy. This manifests into the principle that God should receive the very best. This is born out in a thousand laws, such as the law of dedicating to God the fat from every sacrifice that Israel made, because the fat was the best part of the animal. But thousands of individual laws can be made from a single principle. A law is created with a specific application in mind. The law of the parapet is null and void where there are no flat roofs.

A set of laws is never exhaustive. And the Mosaic Law was not intended to be exhaustive in all necessary applications. Even in a law that seems black and white, done or not done, there is always more than needs to be commanded. The command to build a parapet on the roof did not say how high the parapet needed to be. So if an Israelite built a parapet that was only two feet high, and someone fell off, did the Israelite break that law?

No law will account for all applications, except one. The Law of Deuteronomy 6:5 accounts for all applications. This is why, when the Pharisees asked Jesus what the greatest commandment was, He responded, "'You shall love [Yahweh] your God with all your heart, and with all your soul, and with all your mind.' This is the great and foremost commandment. The second is like it, 'You shall love your neighbor as yourself.' On these two commandments depend the whole Law and the Prophets" (Matt. 22:37–40).

The reason this is the greatest commandment is because it accounts for every action and every motivation. If you perfectly love God, then you will naturally do all things in a righteous and holy manner, without the need for an external set of laws to show you what to do. But as Moses pointed to in Deuteronomy, this is the very problem, because Israel did not have a heart to love God.

A Heart to Love Yahweh

Israel quickly accepted the terms of a covenant with Yahweh. Without hesitation, they said they would do all that was required of them in the Law. They viewed the commands in the same way that the Pharisees did, as a checklist that they could get done. But they did not take into account their wicked heart, that their motivations would be twisted because of their own lusts and selfish desires.

Moses pointed to this again and again in Deuteronomy. Immediately after the reiteration of the Ten Commandments, Yahweh said to Moses, "Oh that they had such a heart in them, that they would fear Me and keep all My commandments always, that it may be well with them and with their sons forever!" (Deut. 5:29). God desired that they would keep His commandments because that meant blessing for them. God was eager to bless Israel, to demonstrate His endless kindness and bounty. But God ultimately will not bless a rebel.

Moses reiterated at the end giving the covenant in Deuteronomy 28 and 29,

> You have seen all that [Yahweh] did before your eyes in the land of Egypt to Pharaoh and all his servants and all his land; the great trials which your eyes have seen, those great signs and wonders. Yet to this day [Yahweh] has not given you a heart to know, nor eyes to see, nor ears to hear. (Deut. 29:2–4)

If Israel was to have a heart that loved God, it must be something that God gave to Israel. Israel foolishly believed they could work their way into favor with God by keeping a checklist. Moses said not only that their heart was wicked, and they could not keep the Law, but also, he said that Yahweh had to be the one who would change their heart of stone into a heart of flesh. This promise of a new heart is given in Deuteronomy 30:6, "Moreover [Yahweh] your God will circumcise your heart and the heart of your descendants, to love [Yahweh] your God with all your heart and with all your soul, so that you may live."

Moses was rightly concerned that Israel would fall away from Yahweh after he died. Moses had always been a mediator between sinful Israel and holy Yahweh. Moses warned the people in Deuteronomy 31:27, "For I know your rebellion and your stubbornness; behold, while I am still alive with you today, you have been rebellious against [Yahweh]; how much more, then, after my death?"

The key to Deuteronomy, with the death of Moses drawing near, was the hope that Yahweh would give Israel a new heart with which they would fear God, keep His commandments, and be an example of holiness.

But as it stood at this point, right before Israel was to go into the Promised Land, after all that has transpired in the wilderness for forty years, Israel was just as rebellious and wicked as the day they came up from Egypt, bringing Egyptian idols with them.

Study Questions:

1. What do you feel you learn about the character of God from the book of Deuteronomy?

2. Why did Moses want the Israelites to remember their past?

3. What was the purpose of the book of Deuteronomy?

4. How do you see the themes of Deuteronomy develop in later books of the Bible?

5. What is the relationship between law and principle?

6. Why is Deuteronomy 6:5 the greatest commandment?

6

JOSHUA

JOSHUA, MUCH LIKE THE Pentateuch, has some amazing stories. Many Christians know the story of the fall of Jericho, when the walls tumbled down. The sun standing still for Israel is also a memorable story.

Rahab was introduced to the Old Testament reader in Joshua, later to reappear in the genealogy of Jesus in Matthew 1:5. Achan and the defeat at Ai is another story depicting the latent sin of Israel.

One might view Joshua as being a positive book in the history of Israel, but many aspects of Joshua can be difficult to understand. By grasping the structure, purpose, and themes of the book we can better understand what was going on.

STRUCTURE

The structure of Joshua is seen in relation to the Promised Land. The first half of the book describes the conquest of the land. The second half of the book explains the distribution of the land.

Joshua 1:1–12:24	The Conquest of the Promised Land
Joshua 13:1–24:33	The Division of the Promised Land

Within this structure, several important narratives guide the entire story of Joshua. Joshua 1:1–5:12 details the crossing of Israel into the Promised Land, which includes sending spies into the land, crossing the Jordan River, and the circumcision of Israel's second generation.

From that point, we can see four major portions to the conquest of the Land. The first was the famous story of Jericho in Joshua 5:13–6:27. This battle for Jericho was a climactic point in Joshua, when God demonstrated His power to defeat Israel's enemies by causing the walls of Jericho to collapse after Israel had marched around the city many times.

The second part of the conquest was not so optimistic because Achan stole some of the loot from Jericho that was devoted to Yahweh. This caused

Israel to be defeated at the hands of their next target, the city of Ai. Upon repentance, Israel, with Yahweh's help, defeated Ai in Joshua 8.

After the defeat of Ai, the important narrative of Joshua 8:30–35 should not be overlooked. Joshua divided the tribes of Israel into two groups and had half ascend Mount Gerizim and the other half ascend Mount Ebal. From these two mountains, they recited the blessings (from Mount Gerizim) and the curses (from Mount Ebal) of the covenant. They renewed the covenant at this time to prepare for the conquest of the entire land.

The third part of the conquest was the southern campaign in Joshua 9–10. In this campaign, the Israelites subdued five Amorite kings as well as several other Canaanite tribes. In this southern campaign we find the story of the sun standing still (Josh. 10:1–15). This incredible story highlights the fact that Yahweh, the Creator of heaven and earth, was fighting on behalf of His people, Israel.

The final part of the conquest was the northern campaign in Joshua 11:1–15. Several tribes were defeated, including the city-state of Hazor, a powerful force in Northern Canaan. Hazor was the only city in the northern campaign that Joshua burned.

Israel, while attempting to drive out and destroy the Canaanite tribes, was not attempting to pillage and plunder, but rather to take over the cities and regions they were fighting for. Only a few select cities such as Hazor were burned. The rest, Israel took over.

Joshua 24:13 states that God gave Israel "a land on which you had not labored, and cities which you had not built, and you have lived in them; you are eating of vineyards and olive groves which you did not plant."

In this way, Israel did not have to build new cities and toil to plant crops but received the produce of the land immediately after the conquest.

The second major division of Joshua is the allotment of the land to the tribes.

Joshua 13:8–33	The allotments to the two and a half tribes east of the Jordan
Joshua 14:1–17:18	The allotments to the two and a half tribes given at Gilgal
Joshua 18:1–19:51	The allotments to the seven tribes given at Shiloh
Joshua 20:1–9	The appointment of the cities of refuge
Joshua 21:1–42	The allotments of the cities for the Levites

After this division of the land, a conflict arose between the tribes on the eastern side of the Jordan and those on the western side, concerning an altar the eastern tribes had built. Joshua 22:1–34 recounts how war was averted over this misunderstanding. Joshua then challenged the leaders of the tribes as well as the people of Israel as a whole in Joshua 23:1–24:28.

The book of Joshua ends with three burials, which marked an important transition for Israel. The death and burial of Joshua is told about in Joshua 24:29–31, the burial of the bones of Joseph is in Joshua 24:32, and in Joshua 24:33, the burial of Eleazar, the son of Aaron, the high priest of Israel.

After Joshua's death, no successor was named, as when Joshua took over for Moses. Israel had given up all ties to Egypt with the bones of Joseph being buried; they had no leader over all the tribes, and their most important religious figure died as well. The question was how the people would respond, which is answered by the book of Judges.

Purpose

Much like the structure, the purpose of Joshua is connected to the Promised Land. Israel had not fixed their heart problem, which Moses pointed out in Deuteronomy. But Israel did have several successes in the book, and Yahweh fought on Israel's behalf.

> **Joshua purpose statement:** With the help of Yahweh, Israel partially conquered the Promised Land and divided the land among the tribes of Israel.

As we will explore in the themes, the question is whether the promise that Yahweh made to Abraham that his descendants would inherit the land was fulfilled in Joshua.

Themes

The themes of Joshua also center around the Promised Land. The land itself is a key theme. Israel's obedience (chapters 1–6, 8, 10–14, 20–21) and disobedience (chapters 7, 9, 15–17, 22–24) are also seen throughout the book. The Law continued to play an important role with the example of Joshua as one who showed himself to be faithful to the Law (Josh. 1:7 and 24:15). Yahweh also continued to show Himself faithful by fighting on behalf of His people.

The Land

Yahweh is a God of faithful covenant love. God always keeps the promises that He makes. Yahweh promised Abraham that his descendants would inherit the land of Canaan. Specifically, Genesis 15:18 gives the borders of this Promised Land, from "the river of Egypt as far as the great river, the river Euphrates." The "river of Egypt" could refer to either the Nile River or the Wadi of Egypt, which is in the Sinai Peninsula (see Ezekiel 48:28 for mention of the brook of Egypt). In either case, the Euphrates River is clearly identifiable. This was a major portion of land, much more than the Israelites conquered in Joshua.

Joshua 21:43–45 explicitly says that the Lord gave Israel all the land He swore to Abraham, Isaac, and Jacob. There was not a piece of land that was not open for the taking because God had fought for Israel, and no enemy could withstand Israel.

However, Israel did not fully take possession of the land. While it was available for the taking, with all of Israel's enemies not able to withstand the power of God, Israel still did not claim the entire Promised Land. Joshua 13:1–7 outlines all of the land which Israel had not taken, even after the northern campaign. This included the regions of the Philistines, the Geshurites, who lived just east of Egypt up to the region of the Philistines, a large portion of the land of the Amorites, and several other regions.

Ultimately, Israel failed to drive out the Canaanites. Joshua 23:13 says, "Know with certainty that [Yahweh] your God will not continue to drive these nations out from before you; but they will be a snare and trap to you, and a whip on your sides and thorns in your eyes, until you perish from off this good land which [Yahweh] your God has given you."

At the end of Joshua, even though God had given all the land to Israel, they failed to take possession of all the land, but instead decided to stop their campaigning and dwell together with many of the Canaanite tribes, as well as the Philistines.

Obedience and Disobedience

The theme of the land in Joshua is one component of Israel's disobedience. But we see several other examples of both obedience and disobedience throughout Joshua.

The book of Joshua is an opportunity for Israel to reestablish themselves. The first generation of Israel came up out of Egypt with God parting the Red Sea for them. The first generation was meant to go into the wilderness, with all their daily needs met, trusting God and keeping His commands. Even though Israel threatened to do so, there was no going back to Egypt after they crossed the Red Sea.

Likewise, the second generation crossed the Jordan River. God parted the Jordan River for them in Joshua 3. While the Jordan River today is a small river when compared with other rivers of the world, in Joshua's time, the Jordan River would have been formidable.

Job described the Jordan River raging up to the mouth of the Behemoth in Job 40:23. Though it is much reduced now, the Jordan River would have been strong when Israel crossed over. God's name was attached to Israel and all of those in Canaan were afraid of this imposing force bearing down upon them. Those in Jericho trusted in their walls, but they still were wary of Israel. And when the Jordan was stopped up and Israel crossed over, this only exacerbated their fear. Israel was meant to act in a way that brought honor and glory to the name of Yahweh. But their track record for this was not great.

The story of Ai and Achan is important in Joshua. It helps us understand God's work on behalf of Israel. God showed great grace to Israel, fighting on their behalf. But God cannot abide with sin. When Jericho fell, God demanded that the entire city be devoted to Him. No one was allowed to take any loot, because God was the one who destroyed the city.

Everything was to be destroyed. However, Achan hid valuables that he had collected from Jericho. Because of this, Israel lost its next battle with Ai, a battle that should have been an easy victory.

However, Joshua showed his extraordinary leadership in this situation. Joshua 7:6–9 tells of Joshua's response to the defeat of Israel. He immediately prayed to Yahweh, appealing to the great name of Yahweh, which was forever linked with Israel. God revealed the hidden sin of Achan.

The consequences were necessary and severe. Achan and his whole family were stoned to death by the people of Israel, and all that he possessed was destroyed. All was buried under a heap of stones as a monument to those who would not follow the instruction of Yahweh (Josh. 7:26).

Achan's disobedience ended in judgment, and Israel was able to continue with the conquest. However, all through Joshua we see latent sin and disobedience of Israel. One key passage in Joshua is the final charge of Joshua to Israel. In Joshua 24:14, Joshua exhorted Israel to put away the idols they had brought from Egypt.

Imagine Israel, walking through the Red Sea with the power of God on display. Imagine Israel being fed manna in the wilderness for forty years.

Imagine each Israelite family seeing the glory of the Lord on Mount Sinai and seeing the judgment of the Lord on those who disobeyed and rebelled against Him. But then imagine that those Israelite families were hoarding Egyptian idols, passed down to them from the first generation.

This was the indictment of Joshua against the people. After all that Yahweh had done for them, they were still clutching the idols of Egypt, which their fathers should not even have brought out of Egypt.

This shows the disobedience of Israel throughout Joshua. While there are bright spots—times when Israel renewed the covenant and attempted to purify themselves—they were never wholeheartedly devoted to Yahweh.

Joshua stands as a bright example of one who was faithful to God, just as Moses had been. But the hearts of the people were still wayward, and this would lead to great disaster when they no longer had a leader who was able to mediate on their behalf before God.

Holy War

One last aspect that must be discussed regarding Joshua is the idea of holy war. There is an ethical question about the complete annihilation of the Canaanites. Yahweh commanded that the Canaanites be destroyed. Deuteronomy 20:17 says, "But you shall utterly destroy them, the Hittite and the Amorite, the Canaanite and the Perizzite, the Hivite and Jebusite, as [Yahweh] your God has commanded you."

That command was at least partially carried out in Joshua. What is the ethical ramification of one nation annihilating another nation, based on their race. Isn't this genocide? Is there such a thing as just war?

This is an important question that needs time and attention. But there are clear biblical answers to this. First, by way of caveat, this must be put in its proper context. God's command for Israel to destroy the Canaanite tribes was just that: A command only for Israel.

Israel was not the church, and no such justification can be extrapolated on a "holy war" such as in the case of the Crusades. Second, by way of caveat, there was no ambiguity in God's command. God commanded Israel to do this while He was dwelling with them. There was no question about God's expectation of what Israel was meant to do.

Deuteronomy 20:18 gives reasoning why Israel was to destroy the Canaanites. It was "so that they may not teach you to do according to all their detestable things which they have done for their gods, so that you would sin against [Yahweh] your God."

Sin is more serious than we realize. Israel was required to destroy the Canaanites so they would not fall into committing the same sins as the Canaanites. Unfortunately, this is exactly what happened. Israel fails to drive out the Canaanites, and Judges tells us the awful ramifications of this.

The sin of a group can become so severe that the only outcome is destruction. This was seen with Sodom and Gomorrah in Genesis 19. The same is true of the Canaanites.

Deuteronomy 7 also reiterated that Israel was to destroy the nations living in the Promised Land, not intermarrying, or interacting with them at all. Israel was a holy people, selected by God to be His special possession (Deut. 7:6). The sin of the Canaanites was serious enough, and Israel's holiness was serious enough, that it demanded the annihilation of the Canaanites.

Study Questions:

1. What does Joshua teach us about God's faithfulness in keeping His promises?
2. How can we properly understand God's command to the Israelites to destroy the Canaanite nations?
3. Why was the land of Israel so important? Why was it important for Israel to have the land God promised them?
4. What does the book of Joshua end with, and why is this significant?
5. What is the story of Achan meant to teach us?
6. What were Joshua's final words to Israel, and what do they tell us about Israel's heart?

7

JUDGES

THE TIME FRAME OF Judges is from the death of Joshua c. 1390 BC to the death of Samson c. 1055 BC. This is a dark period in the history of Israel. Joshua ended with both the deaths of Joshua and of Eleazar the son of Aaron, the high priest.

Israel had lost both their political leader and their spiritual leader. Joshua charged the people to keep the covenant and obey Yahweh with his own example before his death in Joshua 24:15. With no leader over them, it was now down to the individual tribes, clans, and families to follow Yahweh.

At this point in the history of Israel, we start to see major divides between the tribes. They began to see themselves as independent, rather than as a subset of Israel. The tribes began to war against each other. But the tribes also saw this as a problem, which is why in Samuel, they asked for a king who would unite them again.

STRUCTURE

The structure of Judges is based on the individual judges. There are also bookends which highlight the disobedience of Israel.

Judges 1:1–2:10 tells several stories about the leaders of Israel. Joshua's death was recorded in Judges 2:8. Both Caleb and Joshua were depicted as faithful men who served Yahweh, and they kept Israel from slipping into total wickedness.

As long as the leaders of the second generation were alive, Israel maintained some level of godliness. But Judges 2:10–11 says, "And there arose another generation after them who did not know [Yahweh] nor yet the work which He had done for Israel. Then the sons of Israel did evil in the sight of Yahweh and served the Baals."

This starts the cycle of disobedience, oppression, repentance, deliverance, restoration, and then disobedience again.

Judges 3:7–11	Othniel as judge
Judges 3:12–31	Ehud as judge
Judges 4:1–5:31	Deborah as judge
Judges 6:1–8:32	Gideon as judge
Judges 8:33–9:57	Abimelech as king
Judges 10:1–12:7	Jephthah as judge
Judges 13:1–16:31	Samson as judge

Several minor judges also ruled, but little is said about them. This includes Shamgar, Tola, Jair, Ibzan, Elon, and Abdon.

It is also important to note that the judges overlapped chronologically. The period of the judges is about 325 years in total, leading into the time of Samuel and then Saul and David. In fact, Samuel himself was considered a judge. But before Samuel, more than one judge could rule at a time.

Likewise, the oppressors of Israel, usually arising from tribes Israel should have driven out of the land, could subjugate a particular region of Israel. Not every oppressor subjugated all the Israelites.

The end of the book tells several horrific stories that highlight the wickedness of Israel. This is from Judges 17–21. We will examine this end section shortly, but suffice it to say that the point of the section is to say that Israel became more wicked, even, than the Canaanites whom they drove out.

PURPOSE

While Joshua had many positive stories about Israel, Judges is bleak. The leadership of Israel, starting with Moses and moving to Joshua, truly stood in the gap for Israel, holding them back from complete wickedness.

Now that the leadership was gone, very little acted as a tether line for Israel. But the positive note throughout the book is that God continued to raise up judges who helped Israel throw off her oppressors.

> **JUDGES PURPOSE STATEMENT:** God raises judges to guide and protect Israel, even though Israel's complete failure showed that they were worse than the people they drove out.

Themes

The theology in Judges is rooted in the narratives. These stories are examples of the spiritual state of Israel for the reader. They tell us not only of the judges, but also the cycles of Israel's disobedience, subjugation, repentance, and restoration.

Another key theme that we need to see in judges is the brutality with which Israel is described. Unfortunately, the word "brutality" is appropriate in these stories. Also, the Spirit of Yahweh and the Angel of Yahweh are key characters to see in the narratives.

The Judges

While we may be tempted to think that the judges were people devoted to Yahweh, that is not the case. We can even see a turning point in Judges where things get worse.

The first judge mentioned was Othniel, who was the younger brother of Caleb. He delivered Israel from a Mesopotamian king, Cushan-rishathaim. There were still vestiges of the old leadership aiding Israel. Othniel is viewed in a positive light, especially since he came from Caleb's family.

The next judge was Ehud, who killed Eglon, the fat Moabite king. The memorable story of Ehud killing Eglon was followed by Ehud leading Israel to victory over 10,000 Moabite warriors. Ehud was described as courageous and eager to drive out the Moabites. But the courage of Israel began to falter after Ehud.

Deborah and Barak were the next judges of Israel. Deborah called on Barak to stand up to the Canaanite king Jabin and his military commander, Sisera. But Barak did not have the courage to do this alone, so he asked if Deborah would go with him.

Together they routed the army of Sisera, but Sisera was killed by Jael, the wife of Heber, taking the glory of Israel's victory away from Barak. Even though Barak did not show the courage that Ehud had, he was still viewed in a positive light.

The turning point was Gideon who judged next. Gideon was depicted as timid and unwilling to fully trust Yahweh to deliver Israel. The Midianites were oppressing Israel when the angel of the Lord went to Gideon.

Gideon was trying to hide grain from the Midianites in a winepress, hoping he would not be discovered. While Gideon was hiding, the angel of the Lord greeted him and called him "O valiant warrior" (Judg. 6:12). Gideon responded by saying that his clan was the weakest in Manasseh, and that he was the weakest in his father's household. Gideon demanded a sign to verify that he was being sent by God. When the first sign did not convince him, he demanded another. When God commanded him to tear down his father's altar to Baal and his Asherah pole, Gideon did so, but only during the night.

God also winnowed down the men who came out to fight against Midian from 22,000 to 300. This was just to show that it would be God who was delivering the Israelites from Midian, not Gideon. Midian was defeated in the night because the Lord threw them into confusion, and they killed each other.

After the victory, the Israelites tried to make Gideon their king, which he rightly refused (Judg. 8:22). But Gideon collected a large amount of gold as payment for his victory, which he turned into an idol. Judges 8:27 says that all Israel whored after this idol, and it became a snare to Gideon and his entire family. Gideon as judge was the turning point in the book.

Abimelech came after Gideon. He was actually the son of Gideon. And surprisingly enough, his father, Gideon, named him "My father is king," the meaning of Abimelech in Hebrew. While Gideon technically refused to become king, he certainly viewed himself in that way.

After Gideon's death, his son tried to become king. In order to establish his "kingship," he got the city of Shechem to follow him, then he went to his father's house and killed all of his brothers, except the youngest who escaped. This youngest brother, Jotham, was the instrument God used to drive a wedge between Abimelech and the people of Shechem, until finally, Abimelech was killed in battle. Abimelech's actions fragmented Israel, leading to a civil war among the tribes.

Jephthah was the next judge. Jephthah was a hired mercenary who led the people to victory against the Ammonites. Jephthah made a rash vow to Yahweh that if he had victory against the Ammonites, whatever came from the door of his house to greet him upon his return would be sacrificed as a burnt offering. His only daughter came out to greet him upon his return. This wicked vow led Jephthah to sacrifice his only daughter.[1] This was not the only case of the evil of human sacrifice in the Old Testament, and it is a testimony to the perversity of Israel at this time.

Samson, as the final judge, highlighted the lack of leadership, which Israel suffered. The Spirit of the Lord would come upon Samson at times,

1 Many scholars insist that Jephthah did not sacrifice his daughter but dedicated her to Yahweh, meaning she would never marry.

giving him great strength. But Samson's inner strength was lacking. He could not rid himself of his lusts, which caused his downfall to Delilah and the Philistines.

Samson, who was meant to be a great leader of Israel, being set apart even from his birth by a Nazirite vow, had no self-control and ultimately paid for this with his life. Samson's life ended as a blinded man who pushed over the columns of a Philistine temple, killing many Philistines, but also killing himself.

The judges of Israel were viewed positively at the beginning of the book, but over time, they became worse and worse, lacking courage, fidelity to Yahweh, and even a proper understanding of what God required of His people.

The Cycle

Unfortunately, the purpose of Judges is to show the wickedness of Israel. This is clearly seen in their cycles of disobedience. The Pentateuch also depicted Israel in cycles of disobedience, but the pattern was especially clear in Judges. The phrase "then the sons of Israel did evil in the sight of Yahweh" began the cycle (Judg. 2:11; 3:7; 3:12; 4:1; 6:1; 10:6; and 13:1). This is accompanied with a description of their evil, usually following after Canaanite false gods.

This leads to God's punishment of Israel in the form of subjugation and forced servitude to another nation or tribe. The Israelite people cried out in their distress, and Yahweh heard them, remembering His covenant. Yahweh raised a judge to lead and restore Israel, throwing off their oppressors' yokes. But just as quickly as Israel was restored, they turned back to other gods.

This cycle happened again and again throughout Judges. And as the book continued, the judges themselves degraded into wickedness. By the end of the book, neither Israel nor her leaders followed Yahweh. Israel was depicted as being worse than the Canaanite tribes.

The brutality of the book is apparent. The stories in Judges, combined with those right before Israel went into captivity in Babylon, are the lowest moral points of Israel's history. Perhaps the most horrific story in Judges is that of the Levite and his concubine in Judges 19. Both this story and the previous one concerning the tribe of Dan and their hired Levite show that the Levites, far from being the spiritual leaders they were commanded to be, were more like gurus for hire. They were willing to go with whomever would give them the most money, acting as good-luck charms.

The story of the Levite and his concubine takes place in Gibeah, which was one of the cities of the tribe of Benjamin. The unnamed Levite had a concubine who ran away from him back to her father. The Levite proceeded to bring her back, going to her father's house to retrieve her.

On the way back from her father's house, they spent the night in the main square of the city of Gibeah. The story is told in such a way that it is meant to reflect on Sodom and Gomorrah and the angels Lot invited to his house after they spent part of the night in the city square.

An unnamed man took the Levite and his concubine into his house. With similar phrases to Sodom and Gomorrah, the story says certain worthless fellows of the city banged on the door, wanting to have relations with the Levite.

The unnamed man, much like Lot in Genesis, begged them to not do this. However, instead of the angels blinding the wicked men, as in Sodom and Gomorrah, the Levite exchanged his concubine for his own life. She was killed by the men of Gibeah and left on the doorstep in the morning.

The Levite, showing no remorse, took her body with him back home and told the rest of Israel what happened. Israel, even wicked Israel, responded, "Nothing like this has *ever* happened or been seen from the day when the sons of Israel came up from the land of Egypt to this day" (Judg. 19:30). Israel had become worse than those who were in Canaan before.

But even through all these wicked cycles of Israel, Yahweh continued to preserve His people. Not one of the tribes of Israel was annihilated, as were many Canaanite peoples. Yahweh continued to be faithful to His promises made to Abraham, Isaac, and Jacob, even though Israel gave Yahweh no reason to not annihilate them.

The Spirit of Yahweh and the Angel of Yahweh

Two final points should be made about the text of Judges. Several times throughout the book, both the Angel of Yahweh and the Spirit of Yahweh are mentioned.

The Spirit of Yahweh empowered many of the judges for service. This empowering for service was not always coupled with holiness. For example, the Spirit of Yahweh would come upon Samson (13:25; 14:6; 14:19; 15:14), giving him great strength. However, this was not an indication that Samson was acting in a holy manner. Samson, the last judge in the book, was described as a wicked man who only followed his own lusts until the end of his life, when he sacrificed himself in the Philistine temple.

The Spirit of Yahweh also came upon Othniel (Judg. 3:10), Gideon (6:34) and Jephthah (11:29). This will also be seen in the books of Samuel with King Saul. But the Spirit coming upon someone for service should not be mistaken for salvation or holiness, as in the case of the Holy Spirit indwelling the believer in the New Testament.

The Angel of Yahweh was also a crucial character in Judges. The Angel of Yahweh said in Judges 2:1 that He brought out Israel from Egypt and that He swore promises to the patriarchs and made a covenant with them. The Angel of Yahweh was spoken of in Deborah and Barak's song (5:23).

The Angel of Yahweh visited Gideon. Very interestingly, the Angel of Yahweh and Yahweh Himself were interchanged in this narrative. The Angel of Yahweh visited Gideon and spoke with him (6:11). Within the conversation, the text simply says that Yahweh was speaking with Gideon (6:16). After the Angel of Yahweh departed, Gideon exclaimed that he would die because he saw the Angel of Yahweh face to face (6:22).

In Judges 13:19, the Angel of Yahweh accepted the sacrifice of Manoah and his wife, the parents of Samson. The Angel of Yahweh was shown to be Yahweh Himself. This is an example of Christophany in the Old Testament.

Even though the book of Judges reveals great wickedness in Israel, the mention of both the Spirit of Yahweh and the Angel of Yahweh points to the truth that God was continuing to work with His people and would be ultimately faithful to them.

Study Questions:

1. What was "the cycle" and what does it tell us about Israel's heart condition?
2. Were all the judges of Israel good? Why did God choose to use judges who were not truly followers of Yahweh?
3. What can we learn about the emphasis on the Spirit of Yahweh and the Angel of Yahweh in Judges?
4. What was Samson's biggest fault, and why was so much time dedicated to Samson in Judges?
5. Who was the first self-proclaimed king of Israel? What happened to him?
6. Was Gideon a true follower of Yahweh? What was the end result of his judgeship?

8

Ruth

RUTH IS A LOVELY STORY amid a dark time. In our English Bibles, Ruth is placed after Judges, even though this is not the order of books in the Hebrew Old Testament.

Ruth was moved after Judges because Ruth was set in the period of the judges. The date of events is c. 1125–1100 BC, which was immediately after the period of the Midianite oppression of Israel (c. 1165–1125 BC). However, thematically, it should be understood considering both Proverbs 31 and the Song of Songs. Ruth should really be understood as an illustration of the Proverbs 31 woman. And Solomon, writing Song of Songs, also points to finding a godly woman as a wife.

The theme of finding a godly wife is throughout Proverbs (see especially Proverbs 18:22). Ruth is that illustration that Solomon had in his mind. Ruth was Solomon's great-great grandmother. And this fact is not lost on the book, which ends with an important genealogy.

Structure

The name Ruth makes the book seem as though it is centered around the character named Ruth. Ruth is an important character in the story, but perhaps not the central character. Both the Hebrew Old Testament and the Septuagint have named the book "Ruth." But the book seems to be structured around Naomi.

Ruth 1:1–5	Naomi emptied
Ruth 1:6–22	Naomi's daughters-in-law: one departs, and one remains
Ruth 2:1–23	Ruth leaves Naomi
	Ruth's request
	Boaz's response
	Ruth returns to Naomi

Mahlon, and Chilion all died, leaving Naomi and her two daughters-in-law bereft.

At this point, Naomi questioned whether God intended them good or not. She returned to Israel with Ruth, but Orpah, her other daughter-in-law, chose to go back to her family. Upon her return to Israel Naomi said God had dealt bitterly with her, so she had everyone call her Mara, meaning "bitter," instead of Naomi, which means "pleasant."

At this point, many people might question the sovereignty of God. Elimelech might not have made the best decision in leaving Israel and moving to pagan Moab. But how does this book show God's sovereignty?

The book makes innocuous comments about timing. For example, it just so happened that Naomi returned to Israel during the period of the barley harvest (Ruth 1:22). And it just so happened that Ruth decided to glean grain for food for them both, since they had no protection or provider (2:2). And it just so happened that Ruth stumbled onto the field of Boaz who was Naomi's closest kinsman redeemer (2:3). And it just so happened that Boaz decided to check on his field hands that day (2:4).

Ruth is sprinkled with comments about how things were coming together in particular ways for Naomi and Ruth and Boaz. This all was an appeal to the sovereignty of God who was orchestrating these events to bring about His purposes. Ruth acted in a godly way, clinging to her mother-in-law and committing to follow Yahweh rather than the Moabite gods (1:16). Boaz acted in a godly way by showing kindness to the destitute (2:8) and giving Ruth and Naomi protection when they had none. And Yahweh was blessing his faithful people, even when they did not see how He was sovereignly working.

The Line of David

Ruth is a short story that tells us something important about God's sovereignty. Even in a time such as the judges, when Israel exercised their worst forms of paganism and debauchery, God worked to bring about His good plan for Israel.

Ruth and Boaz were married, and God soon blessed them with a child. Naomi, who had returned to the land of Israel empty, was now filled up with blessing, having a godly daughter-in-law, a godly provider in Boaz, and a newborn grandson named Obed. While it may seem peculiar to end the book with a genealogy, this genealogy brings everything into focus and answers the question about how God sovereignly orchestrated these events.

Obed was the father of Jesse, and Jesse was the father of David. Ruth actually picks up from Genesis 38 with the birth of Perez and Zerah. Perez and Zerah were twins born to Judah and Tamar. Genesis 38 is another story that showed God working sovereignly, in spite of the wickedness of Judah, to bless His people. From Judah to Perez, and eventually from Perez to Obed, Jesse, and David, God was working His plan. At this point, it is unclear what further plan God would have with David, but that will become apparent in short order with the book of Samuel.

One last note to make on the genealogy concerns Deuteronomy 23:3–6. This passage gives a command against Moabites saying, "No Ammonite or Moabite shall enter the assembly of [Yahweh]; none of their *descendants,* even to the tenth generation, shall ever enter the assembly of [Yahweh]."

Ruth, as a Moabitess, would be included in this. But we see God's kindness in dealing with Ruth. We might say that Ruth is ten generations after the Deuteronomy passage is given, but it is better to see Ruth as an act of God's kindness toward those who are outside of Israel.

This is also seen in God's gracious dealings with Rahab, a prostitute living in Jericho. Those who were outside of Israel, at times were depicted as better worshippers of Yahweh than those inside Israel. Ruth was linked up with the Proverbs 31 woman and also Song of Songs. She was an example of godliness and dependence upon Yahweh. Yahweh repays that by blessing Ruth during her life, but also blessing her in ways that she would not know during her life. Ruth and Rahab were directly in the line of David and ultimately in the line of Christ. This demonstrates God's kindness in ways that we would not even anticipate.

Redemption

The last theme we will examine in Ruth is the idea of redemption. We have already spoken about God's redemption of Israel, buying them back from the land of Egypt. Naomi and Ruth were in a desperate spot. The culture at that time did not look favorably upon women who lived on their own. Unfortunately, women who had no male protector would fall through the cracks, often being forced to beg or worse. Naomi, upon the death of her husband and sons, realized this terrible plight. She had no way to provide an income for herself, let alone for Ruth.

The provision that was made for this kind of situation was the kinsman redeemer. It would be the responsibility of the closest male relative to take care of Naomi and Ruth.

Boaz was actually not the closest male relative. Another man was closer in relation to Naomi, but his name is not even given in the text of Ruth. He turned down his responsibility to provide for Naomi and Ruth. Initially he said that he would be the kinsman redeemer, but upon being reminded that he would also have to care for Ruth, he said that he would not be the redeemer. Boaz stepped in and took his place. Boaz married Ruth, provided for Naomi, and God blessed Boaz and Ruth with a son.

This godly act by Boaz is an example of redemption by his stepping in and taking care of those who were destitute, those who could not find their own way out of a difficult situation. Boaz was not only in the line of Christ, but he was an excellent example of a redeemer who takes care of those God had entrusted to him.

Study Questions:

1. What is important about Ruth being placed in the period of Judges?
2. What is the main focus of the book of Ruth?
3. What does the book of Ruth tell us about God's sovereignty?
4. What role does Naomi play in the book of Ruth?
5. Why does Ruth end with a genealogy?
6. What does Ruth teach us about redemption?

9

1 & 2 Samuel

THE BOOK OF SAMUEL, dividing into First and Second Samuel in the Septuagint, tells of the important period of Israel's history from the birth of Samuel c. 1110 BC to the old age of David c. 970 BC.

The book of Samuel is filled with interesting characters. Certainly, the central characters are Samuel, Saul, and David. But many other characters appear in the stories, including Bathsheba; Eli the priest; Jonathan, Saul's son; Goliath; Abigail; and many more. The book of Samuel is rich with characters. But the characters all play an important part: to show God's work with His people Israel.

Structure

The structure of Samuel is not as prominent as it is in other books, such as Genesis. But upon digging deeper, we can see the structure and how it plays an important part in telling us the theology and central focus of the book. As mentioned previously, Samuel is comprised of narratives that speak about important characters such as Samuel, Saul, and David. But Samuel is not entirely narrative. This helps to show the structure. Samuel is bookended by two songs.

The first song is Hannah's Prayer. Hannah was the mother of Samuel, but before Samuel came, Hannah had trouble getting pregnant. She was worried that she would not be able to have any children. And to make matters worse, her husband, Elkanah, had another wife, an unfortunately common practice at the time.

The reality that Elkanah had two wives brought much tension and strife into the family. Peninnah, Elkanah's second wife, knew that Elkanah loved Hannah more than he loved her. And Peninnah was able to have children, which she lorded over Hannah. Hannah, in her sorrow over being barren, would go to the Tabernacle and pray to Yahweh for a child. Hannah vowed that if Yahweh would give her a child, that child would be dedicated to

Yahweh. Yahweh answered Hannah's request and gave her Samuel, who at a young age went to live with Eli the priest to be dedicated for service to Yahweh. Hannah's prayer was her response to the kindness of Yahweh to give her a child.

The themes in Hannah's prayer are important. She spoke about Yahweh's uniqueness in that He is a God who can answer prayer. The low are exalted, and the exalted are brought low. Yahweh is able to lift the needy up from despair because Yahweh created the world, owns everything, and is able to bless whomever He desires. And Yahweh takes pleasure in lifting up those who are downtrodden.

Hannah ended her prayer by saying, "He will give strength to His king, / And will exalt the horn of His anointed" (1 Sam. 2:10). This was an important statement for Hannah to make, because at that time, Israel did not have a king. It was still the period of the judges. The only person who attempted to become king was Gideon's son, Abimelech, and that was a complete disaster that caused civil war among the tribes.

But Hannah was looking forward to a king who would rule over Israel, and not only that, she linked the idea of this future king with God's Anointed One, also known as the Christ. This story and the emphasis on Hannah's prayer start the book of Samuel, and David's song ends the book of Samuel.

Second Samuel 22 is David's song of deliverance. It is a very close rendition of Psalm 18. Psalm 18 tells us that David wrote this when "Yahweh delivered him from the hand of all of his enemies and from the hand of Saul." So this is chronologically out of place. David wrote this after the episode of Saul's death. But that was many years before David was an old man, which is the case at the end of Samuel.

So Second Sam. 22 was taken out of chronological order and placed near the end in order to bookend the book of Samuel. This intentional structure reveals the focus of the book. David's song and Hannah's prayer have much in common. Second Samuel 22:51 is especially important, *"He* is a tower of deliverance to His king, and shows loving-kindness to His anointed, to David and his descendants forever."

Both Hannah and David ended their songs with a mention of a king over Israel and God's Anointed One. David also included in the last phrase, "to David and his descendants forever." This was new information that was added in Samuel because at the beginning of the book, Hannah had no idea who would be king and where the Anointed One would come from. But by the end of the book, David knew God's promises to him.

This brings us to the heart of Samuel. Second Samuel 7 lies at the center of the book, after Saul died and David became king of first Judah and then of all of Israel. The Davidic covenant was God's promise to David that his seed would perpetually sit on the throne. Just like with the Abrahamic and Noahic covenants, God made important promises to David that had ramifications for thousands of years after David was gone.

We will examine the Davidic covenant in more detail, but we must first see its central place in the structure of Samuel. Understanding that structure can help us to see past just the individual stories of the characters of Samuel to the theology of Samuel.

Purpose

Understanding the structure of Samuel also helps us understand the purpose of the book. Samuel shows us many vivid characters, but as mentioned previously, we cannot just moralize the stories and miss the central point of Samuel. The promises God made to David set up the rest of the Old Testament, focusing on David's line and the tribe of Judah, from whom eventually Christ would come.

> **Samuel purpose statement:** Yahweh establishes a king over Israel, beginning with Saul, but culminating in David and Yahweh's promise to David of a perpetual kingship through David's seed.

Themes

While technically, the book of Samuel starts in the period of the judges, the book is hopeful and forward looking. Judges pointed to the wickedness of Israel in full color. Samuel had many wicked characters in it, such as the two sons of Eli, but there were also shining examples of faithfulness to Yahweh, seen first in Hannah and Samuel. The themes that run through Samuel include the Davidic covenant, the leaders God chose, and the priests and the ark of the covenant.

The Davidic Covenant

The covenants God makes have far reaching ramifications. The Noahic covenant was a promise of time for wicked humanity to repent, no matter how wicked they became. As the wickedness grows, the clock continues to count away, awaiting the time when God will destroy the world not by water as with the flood, but with fire in the culmination of all things.

The Abrahamic covenant promised that Abraham would be the father of a multitude. It also promised that Abraham's descendants would receive the Promised Land. And finally, the Abrahamic covenant promised that through Abraham, all the nations of the earth would be blessed. The Abrahamic covenant opened the door for redemption and renewal, but was still quite vague on how that would come about. Genesis structured itself by narrowing down how God would bless all nations through Abraham. Genesis narrowed down from Abraham to Isaac, not Ishmael. It continued to narrow down from Isaac to Jacob, not Esau. And at the end of Genesis, Judah was the one who stood out in chapter 49.

The Davidic covenant picked up the baton from Genesis and narrowed the focus from Judah to the specific house of Jesse in Judah, and finally to Jesse's youngest son, David. In Second Samuel 7, David, after gaining the kingship and building his palace, asked Nathan the prophet if David should build the Temple for Yahweh. Yahweh's answer was, "[Yahweh] also declares to you that [Yahweh] will make a house for you" (2 Sam. 7:11).

David asked if he should build a house for Yahweh, and Yahweh's reply was that He would instead build a house for David. This house would be David's dynasty. And Yahweh promised, "Your house and your kingdom shall endure before Me forever; your throne shall be established forever" (7:16).

Jeremiah pulled on this theme and prophesied, "'Behold, *the* days are coming,' declares [Yahweh], 'When I will raise up for David a righteous Branch; and He will reign as king and act wisely And do justice and righteousness in the land. In His days Judah will be saved, and Israel will dwell securely; And this is His name by which He will be called, '[Yahweh] our righteousness'" (Jer. 23:5–6). The book of Kings showed multiple dynasties that arose in Northern Israel, but Judah always had a king from the line of David. Even after the deportation and return, Zerubbabel, the ruling prince was from the line of David. And ultimately, Christ is the King who will rule with righteousness and cause Israel to dwell in security.

God's Chosen Leaders

Leaders come and go in Samuel. Eli and his sons are a perfect example of this. Eli was the high priest and was meant to lead the people into righteous living. Instead, Eli passively sat by while his two sons corrupted the Tabernacle, led wicked lives, and rebelled against God's laws. These sons were the ones who were next in line for the priesthood, but God had different plans.

In a vision to Samuel, God revealed that He would put Eli and his two sons to death. Samuel, broken-hearted, reported this to Eli. God said that no sacrifice could atone for the evil of Eli's house (1 Sam. 3:14). Even Eli recognized that God was just in His punishment (3:18). According to God's word, Eli's sons were killed in battle, and Eli also died after hearing the report (4:17–18).

After Eli, Samuel was viewed as the judge, the one who would Israel spiritually. It is interesting to note the comparisons between Moses and Samuel. Both had a remarkable upbringing and a faithful mother, even though they were raised outside the family home. Both shunned the wickedness around them, Moses in Egypt and Samuel surrounded by the unrighteous practices of Eli's sons. Both are described as faithful (Num. 12:7 and 1 Sam. 3:20). Both killed an enemy of Israel with his own hand (Exod. 2:12–15 and 1 Sam. 15:33). Both were not priests but performed priestly duties (Lev. 8:14–29 and 1 Sam. 7:9). Both functioned as important leaders at pivotal times in Israel's history. Other comparisons can be seen, but it is clear that Moses and Samuel were viewed in a similar fashion in the Old Testament.

There is also a theme of God's appointment of leadership in the juxtaposition of Saul and David. Saul was chosen by the people because he was tall and good looking (9:2). David was a bit of a runt, the youngest son of Jesse who spent his days tending sheep in the wilderness. But the juxtaposition of these two was not more evident than in the story of David and Goliath.

In First Samuel 17, Goliath, a giant and a Philistine, taunted the Israelites, who were too afraid to meet him one-on-one in battle. The text says that Goliath defied the ranks of Israel and thereby defied Yahweh (1 Sam. 17:10). Goliath brought reproach on Israel (17:26) and, in his pride, called on Yahweh and Israel to stop him.

Saul, who was supposed to be the leader of Israel, a tall man and a warrior, was only seen sitting behind the front lines in his tent, unwilling to meet Goliath's challenge. David, upon hearing Goliath's taunt against Israel and the name of Yahweh, was enraged. He was so concerned with Yahweh's name being honored that he took up the challenge, not fearing death but facing it full on in battle against a giant.

David displayed the qualities of a godly leader, ready to stand in battle for the honor of Yahweh's great name. Yahweh raised David up as the leader and rejected Saul as king. Samuel had already anointed David in secret (16:13). Yahweh had raised up His leader to shepherd His people, Israel.

The Priests and the Ark of the Covenant

Two final themes are about the priests and the ark of the covenant. The Levites and priests in Judges were not depicted in a positive light. Eli and his sons followed suit in Samuel. Much of the problem was the care and preservation of the ark of the covenant.

The ark of the covenant was crafted right after Israel came out of Egypt, along with the Tabernacle. Upon the ark of the covenant the blood was sprinkled on the Day of Atonement once a year by the high priest. The issue was that in First Samuel 4:4, the Israelites took the "ark of the covenant of [Yahweh] of hosts who sits above the cherubim" into battle as a good luck charm against the Philistines. Israel believed they could use God in a manipulative way to defeat their enemies.

The Israelites were defeated. This was the battle in which Eli's two sons were killed. The Philistines captured the ark, bringing it back to one of their cities in celebration. However, Yahweh struck them with tumors and humiliated their god, Dagon (1 Sam. 5). The Philistines, who were not described as touching the ark, were still in a panic because the hand of God was against them. The Philistines returned the ark to Israel, and the ark was placed in a small city, Kiriath-jearim, for twenty years (7:2).

The next time the ark moves was when David attempted to take it to Jerusalem (2 Sam. 6). One of the men who was helping with this task was named Uzzah. The ark was never to be touched because God's holiness cannot abide with human unrighteousness.

Second Samuel 6:6 says the oxen that were pulling the cart on which the ark was placed stumbled, and the ark teetered. Uzzah reached out to steady the ark and touched it. God killed Uzzah on the spot.

This may seem harsh, but we must understand the theology behind it. God's holiness cannot abide with humanity's sinfulness. The mud would have been a better place for the ark because at least the mud had not rebelled against God, sinning by wicked thought and action. God wanted His people to realize their sinfulness before Him. It was not possible for God's holiness to be tainted in any way. Uzzah, as a servant of the Tabernacle, should have known that from the first day of service.

This is a lesson for us to also take the holiness of God seriously. If we believe that God acted too harshly, then we do not have a high enough view of God's holiness.

Study Questions:

1. What is at the heart of the book of Samuel?
2. What are the stipulations, and what is the importance of the Davidic covenant?
3. How was Samuel compared with Eli and his sons?
4. Why does God make Saul king if God knew that Saul would ultimately rebel against Him?
5. What role did Jonathan play in the book of Samuel?
6. What was the final state of the ark of the covenant at the end of the book of Samuel? What did the history of the ark of the covenant in Samuel tell us about the state of Israel?

10

1 & 2 Kings

FIRST AND SECOND KINGS should be understood together. The book of Kings depicts the height of Israel's power under Solomonic rule, as well as the complete destruction of Israel, both the northern kingdom of Samaria, as well as the deportation of the southern kingdom of Judah. After Solomon, Israel split into two, a judgment from God because of Solomon's rebellion in his later years as king. But Kings is not just a book about kings, but also about prophets. In fact, the prophets may have had more of a role in the book than the kings do. The prophets included well-known names such as Elijah and Elisha, but the prophets also include people who were not even named in the text, but who delivered their message from God.

Structure

Kings is a book of narrative. The structure follows the stories and their emphases. Kings wants to show us a contrast between Yahweh's faithfulness to keep His promises and the Israelites' unfaithfulness. We can see the major structure through the narratives:

1 Kings 1:1–1 Kings 11:43	The United Kingdom: Solomon's Reign
1 Kings 12:1–2 Kings 17:41	The Divided Kingdom: The kings of Judah and Israel
2 Kings 18:1–2 Kings 25:30	The Surviving Kingdom: The kings of Judah

The kings played a central role in the development of the narratives. A list of the kings along with the length of their reigns will prove helpful. It is also important to see that, based on Yahweh's promise to David, there was no dynasty change in Judah, whereas the northern kingdom underwent several changes of ruling house. Those kings in bold represent a usurper who killed the previous king and started a new ruling dynasty of his own.

Kings of Judah	Reign	Kings of Israel	Reign
Rehoboam	17 years	Jeroboam	22 years
Abijah	3 years	Nadab	2 years
Asa	41 years	Baasha	24 years
Jehoshaphat	25 years	Elah	2 years
Jehoram	8 years	Zimri	7 days
Ahaziah	1 year	Omri	12 years
Athaliah (a queen)	7 years	Ahab	22 years
Joash	40 years	Ahaziah	2 years
Amaziah	29 years	Jehoram	1 year
Azariah (aka Uzziah)	52 years	Jehu	28 years
Jotham	16 years	Jehoahaz	17 years
Ahaz	16 years	Jehoash	16 years
Hezekiah	29 years	Jeroboam II	41 years
Manasseh	55 years	Zechariah	6 months
Amon	2 years	Shallum	1 month
Josiah	31 years	Menahem	10 years
Jehoahaz	3 months	Pekahiah	2 years
Jehoiakim	11 years	Pekah	20 years
Jehoiachin	3 months	Hoshea	9 years
Zedekiah	11 years		

PURPOSE

Throughout Kings, the prophets and the kings are in opposition. The kings seek after power and influence, and they often lead the people into greater and greater wickedness. Yahweh's prophets, on the other hand, are destitute and despised, but they remain faithful to speaking forth the prophecies of Yahweh. They warn the people and the leadership that if they continue down this path, Yahweh will discipline them harshly, driving them into captivity. The people and their leaders do not listen. It is this contrast between the prophets and the kings that is at the heart of Kings.

Kings purpose statement: Israel, splitting into Northern Samaria and Southern Judah because of Solomon's sin, fails to follow Yahweh resulting in their deportation in fulfillment of the prophetic word.

Themes

Kings is a fascinating book that starts off quite hopeful with Solomon's reign, but it ends in devastation with the destruction of Jerusalem. The basis for the book of Kings is God's promise to David that He would seat a man on David's throne from David's line. But the question that comes to the forefront right away is how David's line could be perpetual when the kings of Judah were wicked. We will examine two themes that run strongly through Kings to answer this question: the theme of the kings and the theme of the prophets.

The Kings

Kings begins with the last days of David. David was an old man, ready to pass away, and the kingdom was concerned about who his successor would be. In Samuel, David struggled with his son, Absalom, who attempted to grasp control of the kingdom away from David. Absalom was killed in a battle against David by one of David's army commanders. But the question of who would succeed David was not answered in Samuel. Kings begins with this important question on the table.

Normally succession was by the oldest son. Amnon was the firstborn of David. Second Samuel 13 tells the story of Amnon and Tamar, Absalom's sister. Amnon had unrequited love for Tamar and forced himself on her. In retribution, Absalom killed Amnon. First Chronicles 3:1 says David's second born was named Daniel, born to him by Abigail. But no more was said of Daniel in the Old Testament. It is impossible to know what happened to Daniel, but because he was not mentioned again, we may conjecture that he died as a young person. Absalom was the third son. The fourth son was Adonijah. Adonijah was the one who set himself up as king in First Kings 1, assuming that he was next in line for the throne.

As David was lying in his palace ready to pass away, Adonijah invited all the important people of the land to his "self-coronation" party. However, both Bathsheba and Nathan the prophet met with David to convince him to install Solomon as the king. They were able to accomplish their goal, and David died shortly thereafter.

Unfortunately, Adonijah made a power play in First Kings 2, and Solomon had him executed. Succession after a great king is never an easy transition, especially at this time in the Ancient Near East.

Solomon ascending to the throne set the pace for the fulfillment of the Davidic covenant. God visited Solomon and allowed him to make any request of Him. Solomon appropriately asked for wisdom (1 Kings 3).

Wisdom in the context of the Old Testament is somewhat difficult to define. Wisdom does not necessarily equal godliness, but those who are godly do seek wisdom. Wisdom and discernment can be used in improper ways for a person's own selfish ambition. Solomon's wisdom was an important part of Kings that we should not gloss over. First Kings 4:29, 30, 34 says:

> Now God gave Solomon wisdom and very great discernment and breadth of mind, like the sand that is on the seashore. Solomon's wisdom surpassed the wisdom of all the sons of the east and all the wisdom of Egypt. . . . Men came from all peoples to hear the wisdom of Solomon, from all the kings of the earth who had heard of his wisdom.

This is an important description that we need to understand in terms of the Davidic covenant. God promised a perpetual kingship for David; his descendants would sit on the throne. David rejoiced in this, understanding that God was promising more than just descendants to sit on the throne. God was promising that David's throne will "be established forever" (2 Sam. 7:16), but also that God's loving-kindness would not depart from David's house (7:15). A promise of one awful, ungodly king after another perpetually was not an encouraging promise. Not only would there be a king on David's throne, but that King would ultimately be a righteous King. Solomon's reign was meant to point to this fact.

Solomon's reign was depicted as the golden age of Israel. Solomon amassed more wealth than all those who came before him. He built a new palace, which he called "the house of the forest of Lebanon" (1 Kings 10:17). Solomon made silver as common in Israel as stone, and he made cedar as plentiful as the sycamore.

Solomon's fame grew, and kings from all over sought audiences with him. Solomon's greatest accomplishment was to build the Temple. The Lord blessed the construction of Solomon's temple, and at the dedication, the glory of Yahweh dwelled in the Temple. Solomon was initially depicted as the ideal king, seated on David's throne. But it was not to last.

The nation of Israel was constantly changing, and this was also true of Israel's leadership. Just when Israel seemed to be doing well by following Yahweh, they turned away from Him. The king of Israel was the representative for the nation, and Solomon's heart was turned from Yahweh, showing that he was certainly not the righteous King who would ultimately bless Israel and the nations.

Even though Solomon had all the wealth he could dream of and more power than anyone before him, his many wives turned his heart from following Yahweh. Similar to Samson, Solomon's lust was his downfall. He built altars for all of the gods of his foreign wives and offered sacrifices to these false gods—to Milcom and Molech, the gods of the Ammonites; to Chemosh, the god of the Moabites; and to Ashtoreth, the goddess of the Sidonians (1 Kings 11:5–8).

Yahweh appeared to Solomon twice to warn him of this wicked path, but Solomon did not turn from his ways. Therefore, Yahweh promised, "Because you have done this, and you have not kept My covenant and My statues, which I have commanded you, I will surely tear the kingdom from you, and give it to your servant. . . . However, I will not tear away all the kingdom, *but* I will give one tribe to your son for the sake of My servant David and for the sake of Jerusalem which I have chosen" (11:11, 13).

At this point we must also note the book of Ecclesiastes. Ecclesiastes, written by Solomon when he was an old man, acted as his book of confession and repentance. Ecclesiastes was written from the perspective of someone who has tried to gain satisfaction with all the pleasures of the world, and he has found them empty and meaningless.

Solomon had everything that he wanted. Nothing was held back from him, but this did not prevent him from revealing his heart, which was wayward. Ecclesiastes was Solomon's book of wisdom to those who were, just like him, trying to satisfy themselves through the pleasures of the world.

As Yahweh promised, the kingdom of Israel split in two with ten tribes fracturing off from Solomon's son Rehoboam and following Jeroboam, a young upstart. From this point on, Israel would never again be comprised of twelve tribes but would war against each other.

The cycle after this point in Kings, was a cycle of good kings and bad kings, with the latter being much more frequent. From Jeroboam all the way to Hosea, the last king of Northern Israel, none of the Northern Israel kings was described as good. In Judah, a few kings were good and brought about revivals in Judah, namely Hezekiah and Josiah.

Hezekiah's father was Ahaz, who was one of the worst kings in Judah. His wickedness included even burning one of his sons, one of Hezekiah's brothers, to death as a sacrifice to a false god (2 Kings 16:3). Upon ascending to the throne, Hezekiah turned the nation around, getting rid of all the false altars and idols.

Hezekiah was king when Assyria invaded Judah. Assyria desolated king after king in its wake, including many kings of nations surrounding Judah. Sennacherib raised a siege against Jerusalem, but Hezekiah trusted Yahweh for deliverance. Yahweh proved His faithfulness to Judah by sending the angel of the Lord to kill 185,000 Assyrian soldiers in a night. Sennacherib retreated to Assyria, never to make an assault against Judah again.

Josiah, the fifth to last king of Judah, also led a revival, turning Judah back to Yahweh. Josiah ascended to the throne when he was eight years old (22:1).

When Josiah was 26 years old, the book of Moses was discovered in the Temple. This is an amazing story, showing how far the Israelites had fallen from Yahweh. Writings of Genesis through Deuteronomy were in mothballs in a corner of the Temple. The high priest and a secretary of Josiah's found the Torah and read it to Josiah who responded by tearing his clothes and repenting before Yahweh (22:11). Josiah even reinstituted the Passover celebration, which had not been held for many years (23:21).

But, alas, Josiah was the last good king of Judah. The nation became increasingly morally bankrupt after Josiah, leading to their deportation to Babylon by king Nebuchadnezzar.

Nebuchadnezzar invaded Judah more than once. During the reign of Jehoiakim (609–597 BC), Nebuchadnezzar invaded and made Jehoiakim a vassal (24:1). After three years of subjugation, Jehoiakim rebelled, and Nebuchadnezzar invaded and deported the best and brightest of Judah, including Daniel and his three friends. Jehoiachin took over for his father and only reigned three months before Nebuchadnezzar invaded again and took Jehoiachin captive back to Babylon, taking all of the treasures of the Temple along with another 10,000 captives, including the prophet, Ezekiel.

Nebuchadnezzar installed a puppet king over Jerusalem—Zedekiah. But even Zedekiah rebelled. Nebuchadnezzar had had enough. He marched to Jerusalem and destroyed the city along with what was left of Solomon's temple (25). The description of the fall of Jerusalem, prophesied about in Isaiah, Jeremiah, and elsewhere, was horrific. Starvation was rampant and nothing remained in the wake of Nebuchadnezzar's onslaught.

The poorest of the regions around Jerusalem were left. Nebuchadnezzar, after taking his captives back to Babylonia, imported captives from other conquered nations into Judah. These imported people eventually mixed with those who were left behind in Judah, and even Northern Israel, producing the Samaritans, spoken of in the New Testament.

While Kings starts expectantly with the rise of Solomon's great rule, it ends in despair with the complete destruction of Jerusalem and the Temple. However, not all remains lost. Kings ends with a faint flicker of hope, showing that God is faithful to His promises. The last four verses of Kings say that Nebuchadnezzar released Jehoiachin from prison and gave him a seat at the king's table. Even though Jehoiachin was a wicked king, he was still the rightful king in the line of David, based on Yahweh's promises to David. Yahweh had not forgotten His covenant with David. This flicker of hope was fanned into flame in Ezra and Nehemiah.

Prophets and Prophecy

Elijah and Elisha stand as the most prominent of the prophets in Kings. But many other prophets are also in Kings, including Nathan, Ahijah, Shemaiah, Jehu, Micaiah, Jonah, Isaiah, and Huldah, as well as several prophets who are not even named. These prophets stood in opposition to the leadership of both Judah and Northern Israel. Throughout Kings, a battle was waged between the prophets and the political leaders. This was seen especially in the northern kingdom of Israel.

The fight between the prophets and the political leaders came to a climax on Mount Carmel with Elijah and Ahab. King Ahab was the son of Omri who started a new ruling dynasty when he killed Zimri and took his place as king in Samaria. While not much was said about Omri, Assyrian records speak about Israel as the "Land of Omri." Omri was known as a mighty king, and his son Ahab is spoken of extensively in Kings.

Ahab, the spoiled replacement of his father, married Jezebel the daughter of the Sidonian king Ethbaal, whose name says it all. Ethbaal means, "Baal is with him." The level of pagan cultic influence only grew in Samaria with the influence of this new queen. Elijah stood against this and was often in fear for his life.

Elijah was a fascinating character. He was a nobody from a nowhere place who showed up in front of Ahab and said that it would not rain except by his word. Then Elijah left, not to be seen again by Ahab until the height of the drought and famine.

This confrontation led to the narrative of Mount Carmel, where Elijah challenged the prophets of Baal to a dual. Whoever could call down fire from heaven would show that he served the true God. After the Baal prophets' frenzied failure, Elijah prayed simply and concisely, appealing to the name and glory of Yahweh. Yahweh sent down fire from heaven to consume the sacrifice. Elijah subsequently had the people kill all the prophets of Baal, which enraged Jezebel.

Ahab and Jezebel went back and forth with Elijah. They killed Naboth in order to steal his land, and Elijah arrived to pronounce judgment against them. Elijah was eventually taken into heaven in a chariot of fire and replaced by Elisha, who was a thorn in the side of many kings of Israel. Elisha also acted as an enigmatic character. Stories are told of his replenishing the oil of a widow, raising a widow's son to life, healing Naaman of leprosy, and blinding an entire army. Each in its own context, these stories point to the power of Yahweh, the faithfulness of Yahweh's prophets, and the sovereignty of Yahweh in fulfilling His purposes.

Yahweh's prophecies through His prophets always came to pass. One key example will illustrate this well. Israel and Judah allied together to fight against Syria. Before they left for battle, Ahab wanted to ask his own prophets if he would be successful. Ahab's prophets told him he would win the battle, but then Micaiah, a true prophet of Yahweh, told Ahab that he would die in battle (1 Kings 22:17).

Ahab proceeded with Jehoshaphat, the king of Judah, into battle with Syria, but Ahab disguised himself, hoping not to be noticed. The sovereignty of Yahweh is seen in First Kings 22:34, which says, "Now a certain man drew his bow at random and struck the king of Israel in a joint of the armor." A soldier with no intention of killing Ahab was the instrument Yahweh used to fulfill His prophecy. The random shot hit exactly between plates of Ahab's armor, and he died.

Throughout Kings we see example after example of Yahweh fulfilling His word through the mouth of the prophets.

We might say that the prophets ultimately "won." But this was not a victory in a positive sense. Israel was devastated by Assyria, and Judah and Jerusalem were sacked, with the people taken into captivity in Babylonia. The prophets' voices remained, saying, "I told you so."

Yahweh promised that if Israel and Judah rebelled, they would be punished. The punishment was severe. The description of the devastation in Jerusalem is horrific. The same horror can be seen in the sieges of Samaria, the capital of the northern kingdom. Starvation was so rampant that cannibalism took place inside the city (2 Kings 6:28–29).

When the king of Israel heard of this cannibalism, he decided to punish Elisha, who had prophesied that if the people of Israel did not repent, God would judge them. This battle between the prophets and the kings points to the result of rebellion. Just as was promised in Leviticus and Deuteronomy with the blessings and the curses, if Israel did not follow Yahweh, they would be cursed. Because they were bound by their covenant with God, there was no avoiding this fate if they chose to rebel. Because the prophets spoke God's word, they were seen as an unstoppable force in Israel, even when people such as Jezebel and Ahab tried to stamp them out.

Study Questions:

1. What was Solomon's biggest accomplishment, and what was his biggest mistake?
2. What was the relationship between Solomon in the book of Kings, and the books of Song of Songs and Ecclesiastes?
3. What role did the prophets of God play in Kings? How did they interact with all the kings of Israel and Judah?
4. How many dynasties were in the northern kingdom? How many in the southern kingdom?
5. What did the kings of Judah teach us about God's faithfulness?
6. Why did the book of Kings emphasize the faults of each king? Was this meant to point us to the perfect King?

11

1 & 2 Chronicles

In the organization of the Hebrew Scriptures, Chronicles ends the Old Testament. Chronicles falls into The Writings portion of the Old Testament. Chronicles ends with a recapitulation of all human history up to the point of the proclamation of Cyrus. Just as Genesis started with creation and Adam, so also Chronicles starts with Adam and goes to the proclamation of Cyrus to rebuild the Temple. Chronicles is meant to be another retelling of history, with the focus being on the Davidic covenant.

Structure

Chronicles intends to give a history from Adam to the return of Israel to the land, albeit a more condensed history than Genesis through Ezra/Nehemiah. But the structure can be seen in this intention.

Chapters 1–9 are genealogies starting with Adam and going to those who returned from the exile. From First Chronicles 10 to Second Chronicles 9 emphasis is placed on the reign of David and Solomon. The chapters of Second Chronicles 10–36 speak to the reigns of the rest of the Davidic kings. While Kings spent much time talking about northern Israel and the battle between Yahweh's prophets and the political leaders, all of Chronicles emphasizes the Davidic line with minimal attention on the northern kingdom.

This falls in line with the inclusion of those who returned from exile. Chronicles is reminiscent of Leviticus and Numbers with not only the list of the names but also their functions, especially in relation to the temple worship. First Chronicles 3 outlines the descendants of David, going as far as the grandchildren of Zerubbabel, who was the political leader of those who returned from captivity in Babylonia. Based on this listing, it is understood that the writer or writers of Chronicles penned the book after the return of the exiles, with the intention of reinforcing the importance of the Davidic covenant and Yahweh's faithfulness in preserving the line of David.

Purpose

The emphasis on the line of David is at the heart of the book. The exiles had just returned, and they were starting over. They needed to be reminded of God's promises to David. They were not just another nation of people surrounded by other nations. Instead, they were to be separate, distinct, and faithful to Yahweh because Yahweh was faithful to them. They were to not forget His promise of a descendant of David to sit on David's throne forever.

> **Chronicles purpose statement:** Israel is encouraged to hope in the Son of David, who is the culmination of history and who will come to reign over Israel.

Themes

The primary theme of Chronicles focuses on the kings of the Davidic line. Not only this, but the focus narrows to speak about those kings who were good. This is where we need to understand the relationship between Kings and Chronicles. The kings of Judah were placed into two broad camps: those who did what was right and those who rebelled against Yahweh. But as we saw with Solomon, the Old Testament does not try to pigeonhole its characters. Solomon was considered a good king, but he also turned from the Lord in his later years, and then turned back to the Lord at the end of his life. David was considered a good king, but he also had one of his subjects murdered so that he could steal his wife.

Other kings generally placed into the "good" category by Kings are Asa (1 Kings 15:9–24), Jehoshaphat (22:41–50), Joash, also known as Jehoash (2 Kings 12), Amaziah (14), Azariah, who was also known as Uzziah (15:1–7), Jotham (15:32–38), Hezekiah (18), and Josiah (22). Each of these kings was viewed in a largely positive light. But many flaws were still apparent.

Asa got rid of the male cult prostitutes that plagued the land. He removed his own mother from power because she built an Asherah pole. But the text also says that Asa was not wholly devoted to Yahweh.

Asa's son Jehoshaphat was also described as walking in the ways of Asa his father—doing what was right. But Jehoshaphat made a covenant with wicked King Ahab, saying, "I am as you are, my people as your people, my horses as your horses" (1 Kings 22:4).

Amaziah was depicted as doing right, but not like David. He did not remove the high places. Likewise, Uzziah was good, but kept the high places.

Chronicles, in its emphasis on the Davidic line, often gives more detail about these kings. Asa, Jehoshaphat, Joash, Amaziah, Uzziah, Jotham, Hezekiah, and Josiah were all viewed in a positive light. But they were also described as not going far enough in their reforms.

Certainly, Hezekiah and Josiah were viewed well, making sweeping reforms to Judah. But some kind of failure always highlights that these kings are not the One who was promised to come. While the Davidic line was still on the throne, it had not satisfied the expectation of a righteous King who will sit on David's throne.

Both Isaiah 11 and Jeremiah 23 discuss the righteous Branch who would come from the line of David. They contrasted this with the shepherds or leaders of Judah who were destroying the people. Yahweh said that after the people were scattered, He would bring them back and set shepherds over them who would care for them rather than abuse them (Jer. 23:4). Jeremiah 23:5–6 states, "'Behold, the days are coming,' declares [Yahweh], 'When I will raise up for David a righteous Branch; And He will reign as king and act wisely And do justice and righteousness in the land. In His days Judah will be saved, And Israel will dwell securely; And this is His name by which He will be called, '[Yahweh] our righteousness.'"

This promised righteous King is contrasted especially with those evil kings who oppressed the people. But even the good kings failed. Hezekiah, in his pride, allowed the Babylonians to see his treasure before he realized that they were a threat (2 Chron. 32:27–31).

Another failing of the kings revealed throughout Chronicles was their interaction with the Temple. Certainly, the bad kings of Judah were indicted because they polluted the Temple, introducing idols and wicked cultic practices. But even the good kings did not always treat the Temple well.

Uzziah was an important example of this. Second Chronicles 26:1–23 tells the story of King Uzziah who was instructed by the prophet Zechariah. God blessed Uzziah because he feared Yahweh, paying attention to what Zechariah directed. Second Chronicles 26:15 says that he was even an inventor. But when his fame grew and he became strong, he grew proud.

Uzziah grew so proud that he believed he could not only be king, but also take on the role of priest. He attempted to offer incense as only the priests were allowed to do in the Temple. Several righteous priests withstood him and would not allow him to burn the incense.

As Uzziah grew angry about this, Yahweh struck him with leprosy on his forehead (26:19). The priests rushed him out of the Temple, and he lived in isolation as a leper for the rest of his days, with his son Jotham reigning as a regent in his place.

Pride was a common flaw for the good kings of Judah. Whether showing off their wealth, as in the case of Hezekiah or rushing out to battle, as in the case of Josiah or trying to take on the priestly role, as in the case of Uzziah, none of the good kings was the fulfillment of the Davidic covenant in and of themselves.

Chronicles, while still highlighting the failings of David's line, also speaks of the righteousness of David's line, more so than the book of Kings.

Manasseh, Hezekiah's son, was an important example of this. Often, the son of a good king turns out to be an evil king. First Chronicles 33:1–20 tells the story of Manasseh. He was only twelve years old when he became king, which means that Hezekiah would have been forty-two years old when Manasseh was born.

It is unclear why Hezekiah's firstborn son was born so late in his life. But young as he was, Manasseh reigned for fifty-five years from Jerusalem. The text says that Manasseh not only rebuilt all the high places that his father had torn down, but he also erected altars for the Baals and made Asherah poles. He "worshipped all the host of heaven and served them" (2 Chron. 33:3). He even built pagan altars inside the temple of Yahweh. He offered his sons up as burnt sacrifices to the gods in a valley next to Jerusalem; he practiced "witchcraft, used divination, practiced sorcery and dealt with mediums and spiritists" (33:6).

The book of Kings does not speak about the repentance of Manasseh. Kings recounts Manasseh's wickedness, which was the final straw and led Yahweh to pronounce judgment on Judah (2 Kings 21:12–15). Kings does reference the Book of the Chronicles of the Kings of Judah, which recounts more of what Manasseh did.

Second Chronicles 33:10–20 tells the story of Manasseh's repentance. Yahweh brought the king of Assyria against Judah, who carried Manasseh into captivity (2 Chron. 33:11). When Manasseh was without hope, he humbled himself and repented of his wickedness. Yahweh rescued him and brought him again to Jerusalem to be king.

Manasseh, being true to his repentant plea, removed the foreign gods and the idols from the Temple. He restored the altar of Yahweh and reinstituted the sacrifices to Yahweh.

Manasseh's grandson, Josiah, brought revival in Judah. Josiah is the last great king of Judah.

The intention of Chronicles is to show how God worked in the line of David. Even though the good kings were not always good, God was still preserving the line of David. This is shown even with wicked kings who turned back and repented before Yahweh. But the destruction was set and would come upon Jerusalem.

Second Chronicles 36:17–21 speaks about the destruction of Jerusalem. Verse 21 says this was "to fulfill the word of [Yahweh] by the mouth of Jeremiah, until the land had enjoyed its sabbaths. All the days of its desolation it kept sabbath until seventy years were complete."

Israel did not follow Yahweh's command for the Sabbath year of rest. So, while Israel was in captivity, the land got its seventy years of Sabbath rests.

Chronicles ends on the command of Cyrus, King of Persia, to rebuild the Temple. A great deal occurred between the destruction of Jerusalem and the command of Cyrus. Ezra, Nehemiah, Esther, Daniel, and several of the Twelve dealt with this in-between time. So, Chronicles was written with a different intention than Ezra, Nehemiah, Esther, Daniel, Haggai, or Malachi, all of which are set in the time of the exile.

Chronicles was written after the decree of Cyrus to remind those who were returning to the Promised Land of their history. It was a warning to not fall back into the same mistakes and sins seen again and again in Israel's history. God was giving Israel another chance, allowing the people to return to their land. Israel needed to be reminded of their hearts. Did they have a heart to follow Yahweh or not?

This was the same issue that Moses pointed to in Deuteronomy. The writer or writers of Chronicles wanted the exiles to remember where they had come from. Chronicles also reminded exiles of Yahweh's faithfulness to His promises.

The kingdom of Judah had been destroyed, so what happened to the promise of the Davidic covenant? How could this be fulfilled? The book of Chronicles, even by pointing to God's faithfulness to the Davidic line before the exile, showed that God was still working with Israel and would fulfill all His promises.

Study Questions:

1. What was the main focus of Chronicles?
2. Why did Chronicles start with Adam and give genealogies?
3. How was Manasseh described in Chronicles, and did this contradict the book of Kings?
4. Why did Uzziah want to offer sacrifices? Why did he think this was an important and necessary task for a king?
5. Why did Chronicles end with the command of Cyrus, and what does this tell us about the faithfulness of Yahweh?
6. What can we learn about the heart condition of Israel in Chronicles?

12

Ezra & Nehemiah

EZRA PICKS UP RIGHT where Chronicles left off. Chronicles used only two verses to speak of the command of Cyrus, king of Persia, to rebuild the temple in Jerusalem. Second Chronicles 36:23 says, "Thus says Cyrus king of Persia, '[Yahweh], the God of heaven, has given me all the kingdoms of the earth, and He has appointed me to build Him a house in Jerusalem, which is in Judah. Whoever there is among you of all His people, may [Yahweh] his God be with him, and let him go up!'"

There is a question as to how many trips the exiles made back to Jerusalem. Besides Ezra and Nehemiah, two names were mentioned of those who led returns to Jerusalem: Sheshbazzar and Zerubbabel.

Sheshbazzar was named four times (Ezra 1:8; 1:11; 5:14; and 5:16), and he was called the prince of Judah. His father's name was not given. Zerubbabel, on the other hand, was called the son of Shealtiel (3:2).

Whether these were two different people or the same person called by two different names, Ezra recounts that 42,360 people returned to Jerusalem after the decree of Cyrus. Those who returned were mostly poor, with many Jews choosing to stay in Persia.

This set up the story of Ezra, who led his own return after the initial wave. Ezra has a great deal of work to accomplish in Jerusalem. The initial wave of exiles occurred soon after the decree to return went out in 538 BC. Ezra's return was not until 458 BC. The initial returnees were languishing, unable to make progress on the restoration of the Temple and the land.

Structure

We cannot see the structure of Ezra apart from its connection with the Book of Nehemiah. Just as with the Twelve, in the Hebrew, Ezra and Nehemiah are considered as two volumes of the same book. They are connected and should not be viewed separately. The structure of both books depends on the different returns of the exiles.

The first return under the command of Zerubbabel (depending on whether Sheshbazzar and Zerubbabel were different people who led two different returns) is recorded in Ezra 1–6. Ezra 7–10 speaks about the return of Ezra. Nehemiah 1–13 depicts the return under the command of Nehemiah. Ezra and Nehemiah were written c. 420–400 BC. The final deportation to Babylon was in 586 BC. Several Old Testament books were written after the exile but before Ezra/Nehemiah, including Daniel, Esther, and Ezekiel. Daniel, for example, was written c. 535 BC. We can correlate the events of Ezra/Nehemiah to specific years within the Persian period.

Year	Event	Reference
538 BC	The decree of Cyrus	Ezra 1:1–4
537/6 BC	The return under Sheshbazzar; the altar rebuilt	Ezra 1:5–3:6
536/5 BC	The laying of the foundation of the Temple	Ezra 3:7–13
536/5–520 BC	The work on the Temple stopped	Ezra 4:1–5, 24
520 BC	The work on the Temple resumed	Ezra 5:1–6:13
515 BC	The Temple completed; The celebration of Passover	Ezra 6:14–22
486 BC	An accusation concerning the inhabitants of Judah to King Ahasuerus (Esther's husband)	Ezra 4:6
464 BC (?)	A letter of accusation to Artaxerxes	Ezra 4:7
464 BC (?)	A letter concerning the rebuilding of the walls of Jerusalem	Ezra 4:8–23
458 BC	The decree of Artaxerxes; The return of Ezra	Ezra 7:1–10:16
457 BC	The report concerning those with foreign wives	Ezra 10:17–44
446 BC	The report to Nehemiah concerning Jerusalem	Nehemiah 1:1–11
445 BC	The decree of Artaxerxes; The return of Nehemiah; The rebuilding of the wall; The repopulating of Jerusalem; The teaching of Ezra; The celebration of Tabernacles; The confession and covenant of the people; The dedication of the walls	Nehemiah 2:1–13:3
445–433 BC	The first governorship of Nehemiah	Nehemiah 5:14–15
430–423 BC	The second governorship of Nehemiah	Nehemiah 13:4–31

Kings came and went as well within these time periods. Even the book of Daniel has narrative from Nebuchadnezzar, king of Babylon to Cyrus, king of Persia. The narratives of Ezra 1–6 include four successive kings of Persia: Cyrus, Darius, Ahasuerus, and Artaxerxes. Ahasuerus was also called Xerxes and was the husband of Esther. However, the focus was on Artaxerxes and his decrees in Ezra 7 to Nehemiah 13, which is from the period of 458 BC to 425 BC. This is why a conservative date of the writing of Ezra and Nehemiah is c. 420–400 BC.

In discussing the structure, we need to understand the relation between Ezra and Nehemiah. They were not one book originally, which was later divided into two such, as in the case of First and Second Samuel or First and Second Kings. Ezra and Nehemiah are two distinct books, but they are meant to be read and understood together, a volume one and volume two, if you will.

We can see the unity of the books in several different areas. The Hebrew tradition sees them as unified. The themes of the books also align well. Both were concerned about the book of the law (Neh. 8:1 and Ezra 7:6, 10). Ezra was a key character in both, with his reading of the Law in Nehemiah 8. Zerubbabel, the prince who was descended from David, as well as Jeshua the high priest were also key characters. The return of Nehemiah was seen as a necessary wave of exiles after the return of Ezra. Ezra was just concerned with the building of the Temple and Nehemiah with the rebuilding of the wall of Jerusalem.

These books are also distinct. Nehemiah has its own introduction. Interestingly, Ezra told a story in third person, whereas Nehemiah frequently referred to himself in first person voice. Each book has some distinct phrases. Ezra used the phrase "the God of Israel" thirteen times, but it is not found in Nehemiah. It is also important to note that Nehemiah 7 seems to be a reiteration of Ezra 2.

One other key characteristic in Ezra that is not found in Nehemiah is the use of Aramaic. While Israel was in captivity, the people were greatly influenced by the surrounding cultures. Aramaic was taking over as a dominant language, a *lingua franca.* It was the language of commerce, trade, politics, and economics. If you wanted to work and integrate into the world around you, you needed to be able to speak Aramaic. Hebrew was a small language in comparison.

As the Jews lived and worked in Persia, they began to lose the ability to speak Hebrew. Eventually, by the time of Jesus, Hebrew was still preserved, but as a religious language, used predominantly by the religious leaders. It was not forgotten entirely by the people, but it was not the everyday language used. Aramaic had an important place, and eventually Greek began to take over for Aramaic. The letters in Ezra 4:8–6:18 and 7:12–26 were kept in their original Aramaic forms, which is what would have been sent to Persia. Daniel also used Aramaic extensively, with about half of Daniel written in that language.

Purpose

If we see Ezra and Nehemiah as two volumes understood together, then it is appropriate to see one guiding purpose behind their writing. The Temple was in central focus in Ezra especially. The intention of Ezra and Nehemiah was to demonstrate God's faithfulness in bringing the people back from captivity. They were the ones who had rebelled and rightly deserved to be taken into captivity, especially after all the warnings they received from the prophets. The question is whether the people changed while they were in captivity. Did they learn their lesson?

> **Ezra and Nehemiah purpose statement:** Yahweh's continued faithfulness to the Abrahamic covenant meant that Yahweh brought back Israel from captivity to give them another opportunity to be faithful to Him and maintain the Mosaic covenant, especially through the rebuilding of the Temple and reinstitution of the sacrifices.

Themes

Several key themes can be seen throughout both Ezra and Nehemiah that tie the books together. These include the sovereignty of God, the Temple, and the sin and confession of the people. The prayers of Ezra and Nehemiah were also included as a theme.

The Sovereignty of God

The sovereignty of God is a theme in every book of the Bible, but we see it in special ways in certain books. We might say the reader is reminded of the sovereignty of God in special ways.

Ruth is a wonderful example of that. Ezra and Nehemiah are, too. The content of Ezra and Nehemiah points to this in a masterful way. We know that God promised, though the Abrahamic and Davidic covenants, that He eventually would establish His people in Israel with no one to make them afraid. In addition, God's King would reign from Jerusalem, bringing peace. The return was a clear sign that God was still working with His people; He had not forgotten them.

But we also see God's sovereignty in small ways in Ezra and Nehemiah. We may be tempted to gloss over Ezra 1:9–10, for example. These verses say that Sheshbazzar brought back from exile not only a troupe of people but also 1,000 basins of silver, 30 basins of gold, 29 censers, 30 bowls of gold, 410 bowls of silver, and 1,000 other vessels.

Why was this important? Why list these out by number? Because it showed the sovereignty of God. Not only did God sovereignly move Cyrus to give the decree of return, and not only did the Spirit of God move those from Judah, Benjamin, and Levi to return, but God also sovereignly worked in Cyrus so much that he decreed that the vessels that were taken from the Temple be sent back along with the Jews.

These Temple vessels came in and out of the stories of the exile. Daniel recorded that Nebuchadnezzar pilfered many of the vessels from the Temple, vessels that Solomon had made and dedicated for use in the Temple (Dan. 1:2). These vessels were also a key part of the story of King Belshazzar in Daniel 5. Belshazzar gave a great feast for his nobles and decided that they should use the vessels of the temple of Yahweh in their feast. A hand appeared and wrote on the wall that he would be killed that night and his kingdom overtaken. That very night, the Persians overthrew the Babylonians and Israel entered captivity of the Persians instead of the Babylonians.

These Temple vessels were meant to be consecrated and holy. We must remember Numbers 7 and the gifts each tribe gave to the dedication of the Tabernacle, all the instruments and bowls which were dedicated and given. God had not forgotten even the instruments which were to be used in the Temple. Solomon created the instruments for the Temple and dedicated them. They were consecrated to Yahweh, and Yahweh would not leave them behind, even though the Babylonians treated them like any other vessels.

The sovereignty of God is seen in big ways such as in the decree of Cyrus and the return of the people—but also in small ways that we should not miss in the text.

Prayer

Prayer is a central aspect of Ezra and Nehemiah. Both books reflect on the need for Yahweh's people to entreat Him, not only in confession of their sins, but in the way Moses entreated Yahweh, appealing to His name. Ezra prayed throughout the book of Ezra (e.g., Ezra 10:1), but the prayers of Nehemiah were especially highlighted and were written in the first person voice. Nehemiah 1:5–11; 2:4; 4:4–5; 4:9; 5:13; 5:19; 6:9; 6:14; 9:5–38; 13:14; 13:22; 13:29; and 13:31 are all examples of Nehemiah's prayers. Some of them are lengthy, and some are simple, such as Nehemiah 13:14, "Remember me for this, O my God, and do not blot out my loyal deeds which I have performed for the house of my God and its services."

In this case, Nehemiah was telling the story of the book in first person and unexpectedly broke out into prayer. We are able to truly see the heart of Nehemiah, his desire to obey Yahweh, and his desire to see Jerusalem built up again for the glory of Yahweh.

Prayer is an essential theme that shows the intention of those who were leading the Jews back to Jerusalem. Their purpose was not to receive praise for their own name or for their own glory, but because they were concerned about the glory of Yahweh, appealing to His name and His promises to Abraham, Isaac, and Jacob.

The Temple

Jerusalem without the Temple was incomplete. Ezra understood this. Since Israel was bound to the Mosaic covenant, they were required to observe sacrifices and the festivals that Yahweh commanded. The Day of Atonement, the blood sacrifices, even the social interaction of the people were all tied to the Temple.

According to the Mosaic law, the Israelites were required to go up to Jerusalem three times a year during particular festivals. The Temple was at the heart of these festivals as well as the sacrifices made. The first priority for Ezra was the building of the Temple, not the fortifications of Jerusalem. Jerusalem had enemies all around, but the priority remained the same.

After the Temple was built, Nehemiah correctly recognized the need for the wall to be rebuilt, and he led the people to complete the wall in fifty-two days, dividing up the construction work by families into forty-two groups. Nehemiah 4:17 says, "Those who were rebuilding the wall and those who carried burdens took *their* load with one hand doing the work and the other holding a weapon." But all work done on the wall was after the Temple was completed.

The Israelites were in captivity for seventy years, but some of the 42,360 who returned to Jerusalem had been alive at the time of Babylon's invasion. When the foundation of the Temple was completed, Ezra 3:11–13 says:

> And all the people shouted with a great shout when they praised [Yahweh] because the foundation of the house of [Yahweh] was laid. Yet many of the priests and Levites and heads of fathers' *households,* the old men who had seen the first temple, wept with a loud voice when the foundation of this house was laid before their eyes, while many shouted aloud for joy, so that the people could not distinguish the sound of the shout of joy from the sound of the weeping of the people, for the people shouted with a loud shout, and the sound was heard far away.

Those who had seen the first Temple recognized an important difference. The difference was not in materials made or a lack of gold and cedar. The difference was that this second Temple did not have the glory of Yahweh in it. At the dedication of the Tabernacle, Exodus 40:34–38 says the glory of Yahweh descended and filled the Tabernacle. The same occurs at the dedication of Solomon's temple in First Kings 8:10–11. But Yahweh does not fill this Temple; the holy of holies has no presence of the Lord in it. The glory of Yahweh left the Temple before it was destroyed by the Babylonians (Ezek. 10). At that point, the ark of the covenant was only a physical box, no longer bearing the weight of death for anyone who touched it, as in the case of Uzzah in Second Samuel 6:6. In this second Temple, sacrifices were reinstituted, and the Temple again became the central focus of Israel. But those who remembered the glory of Yahweh in Solomon's temple wept.

The Sin and Confession of the People

A final theme to point out is the sin and confession of those who returned to Jerusalem. Yahweh gave the people another opportunity to follow Him. Just as before, they did not have a heart that loved Yahweh. There were bright spots, such as when the returned exiles celebrated the Passover (Ezra 6:19–22). But the people did not know the Law, so Ezra was put in charge of teaching the people the commands of Yahweh.

Even after the reading of the Law, the people did not obey. Ezra was told (Ezra 9) that the people had intermarried with foreigners around them. This was even done by the leaders of Israel and many prominent men (9:2). Ezra's response and prayer was seen in Ezra 9:6–15. He was astounded that the people had so quickly gone back to their old ways. He called the people to repent, and they initially agreed, though they delayed (10:12–14). Eventually, they did separate from the foreigners, and even made a list of those Levites who married foreign women (10:18–44).

This reform did not last. Nehemiah served as governor over the people after this point, and soon realized that the people were breaking the Law. They were not giving the appointed tithes and gifts to the Temple (Neh. 13:10). People worked on the Sabbath as though it were any other day (Neh. 13:15–18). The people returned to intermarrying, even to the point that their children spoke the languages of Ashdod, Ammon, and Moab and not Hebrew (13:23–24).

Nehemiah confronted the people again, warning them that they had sinned just as Solomon had sinned with his many foreign wives. Nehemiah attempted to cleanse the people, similar to Moses in the Pentateuch. But the people's hearts were still hard. They were not able to keep the Law because they did not have a heart to love Yahweh, just as Moses predicted in Deuteronomy. After all his work, Nehemiah was only able to pray, "Remember me, O my God, for good" (13:31).

In Ezra and Nehemiah, we see that the people had not changed, but Yahweh would still remember His promises, His covenants, and those who were faithful to Him.

Study Questions:

1. Did Ezra/Nehemiah paint Israel in a good or bad light?
2. What did Ezra/Nehemiah tell us about God's faithfulness, even down to the minute details?
3. Why do you think that Nehemiah is written for the most part in the first person voice?
4. What can we learn about prayer from the example of Nehemiah?
5. Why was Ezra's first priority the building of the Temple and not the building of the wall of Jerusalem?
6. Why do you think that Israel continually intermarried with nations around them when God forbade it?

13

Esther

THE BOOK OF ESTHER never mentions God's name. This should sound bizarre to us. Even more so, the book does not mention the Temple, Jerusalem, the Law, and does not even mention prayer. Didn't Esther pray to God that He would deliver them from the plot of Haman? This was not recorded. Mordecai and Esther both responded to Haman's plot by fasting, going about in mourning, and putting ashes on their heads. There is no mention of them praying to Yahweh to seek His guidance, His protection, or His favor.

Because of this, some have questioned whether or not Esther should be part of the canon of Scripture at all. But there was a reason for this absence. There is intentionality behind this. We can see this in the structure and purpose of the book.

Structure

Esther has a wonderfully intricate structure. Esther makes use of *chiasm*, which is a literary device where the second half mirrors the first half in an opposite manner. Basically, we can think of it as the story looking at itself in a mirror.

The central focus of the book, based on the structure, is the fact that the king could not sleep on a particular night. This is supposed to seem innocuous, but it is meant to be understood as the Lord working, even when no mention of His name is given.

The cause is not mentioned, but the results speak for themselves. The people of Israel were preserved from complete destruction. God raised up Esther for a particular time. God caused the king to not be able to sleep and for him to have the account of Mordecai read to him. Throughout the whole book we can see the hand of God at work, all behind the scenes.

The outline on the next page will help to show the structure.

A Prologue: Persian festival and ascension of Esther (1:1–2:23)
- **a** The greatness of Ahasuerus; Vashti is deposed (1:1–22)
- **b** Esther is chosen, banquet in her honor; her Jewishness is hidden (2:1–18)
- **c** Mordecai foils the plot to assassinate Ahasuerus (2:19–23)

B Complication: The Jews endangered by their archenemy (3:1–15)
- **a** Haman, archenemy of the Jews, plots to destroy the Jews on Adar 13 (3:1–7)
- **b** Haman persuades Ahasuerus to issue an edict to annihilate the Jews (3:8–15)

C Response: Mordecai's strategic appeal (4:1–17)
- **a** The Jews in Susa lament over the first royal edict (4:1–3)
- **b** Mordecai persuades Esther to appeal to Ahasuerus (4:4–17)

D Development: Esther's first banquet (5:1–8)
- **a** Esther averts death and invites Ahasuerus to attend her banquet (5:1–5)
- **b** Esther's first banquet; she defers her request (5:5–8)

E Centerpiece: The fall of Haman and the rise of Mordecai (5:9–6:14)
- **a** Haman boasts; his wife/friends encourage him to hang Mordecai (5:9–14)
- **b** Turning point: that night the king cannot sleep (6:1–11)
- **a'** Haman laments; wife/advisor predicts his downfall before Mordecai (6:12–14)

D' Consequence: Esther's second banquet (7:1–10)
- **b'** Esther's second banquet; she makes her request (7:1–8)
- **a'** Haman invites his own death when he pleads to save his life (7:9–10)

C' Resolution: Mordecai's strategic appeal (8:1–17)
- **b'** Mordecai persuades Ahasuerus to issue a second edict (8:1–14)
- **a'** The Jews in Susa rejoice over the second royal edict (8:15–17)

B' Denouement: The Jews victorious over their enemies (9:1–19)
- **b'** The Jews are victorious and destroy their enemies on Adar 13 (9:1–5)
- **a'** Esther persuades Ahasuerus to allow Jews to kill Haman's Sons (9:6–19)

A' Epilogue: Jewish festival and ascension of Mordecai (9:20–10:3)
- **c'** Mordecai institutes Purim to celebrate foiling of Haman's plot (9:20–28)
- **b'** Esther authorizes Purim festival; her Jewishness is displayed (9:29–32)
- **a'** The greatness of Ahasuerus; Mordecai is empowered (10:1–3)

Purpose

As mentioned above, the lack of any mention of Yahweh, the Temple, Jerusalem, or prayer points to the purpose of Esther. In a similar way to Ruth, where events were described as being "random," the intention was to show that God was working in all the details to bring about His plan. In the case of Esther, God's plan was the preservation of Israel, even though they were in captivity and not being faithful to Him.

> **Esther purpose statement:** While the Jews, generally speaking, were not faithful to Yahweh while in captivity, Yahweh still protected and preserved them even though they did not call upon Him.

Themes

The themes of Esther are bound up in God's sovereign protection of His people. We are able to see how God foils the plans of wicked men. Haman was the key example of this.

Haman was referred to as the Agagite. He was called the Agagite five times in the book, and this is the only mention of Agagite anywhere in the Bible. But we do know the story of King Agag. King Agag was a king of the Amalekites in the time of King Saul of Israel. God required that the Amalekites, who were originally living in the land of Canaan, be killed so they would not corrupt the Israelites with their false gods.

Saul had just become king and was making war against many people, including the Ammonites, the Edomites, the Moabites, the Philistines, and the Amalekites. Before Yahweh turned against Saul, Saul was winning battles, even over the Philistines. Now this is before the story of Goliath. The Amalakites were another victory that Saul had.

Yahweh commanded Saul to destroy the Amalakites, devoting to destruction all that they possessed. Saul was victorious over them, and he captured their king, Agag. First Samuel 15:9 says, "But Saul and the people spared Agag and the best of the sheep, the oxen, the fatlings, the lambs, and all that was good, and were not willing to destroy them utterly; but everything despised and worthless, that they utterly destroyed."

They disobeyed the command of Yahweh, so Yahweh sent the prophet Samuel to Saul. Samuel confronted Saul and asked him why he did not devote everything to destruction. Because of Saul's greed, Yahweh rejected him from being king over Israel. Samuel's response to Saul was, "The Glory of Israel will not lie or change His mind; for He is not a man that He should change

His mind" (1 Sam. 15:29). Samuel then brought Agag before the people and killed him (15:33). This is the only reference to the Agagite people.

Haman is identified as being descended from Agag. With First Samuel 15 as a background, we can see the hatred that Haman had for the people of Israel, the reason why he wanted them all to be destroyed. However, just as with Balaam and Balak, what one man intended as evil against Israel, Yahweh intended for good and foiled the plans of man.

Haman's plans not only included destroying of Israel, but also his own exaltation. As an advisor to the king, a king who was depicted as being easily manipulated and self-centered, Haman had the advantage of gaining all the power he wanted. But it just so happens that Yahweh allowed Mordecai to save the king's life, foiling a murder plot by two relatively unknown characters.

Haman's maneuvering could not best God's plans. From the start of Haman's plot, it was doomed for failure. Haman's own neck was bound for the gallows that he built for Mordecai. Haman's power plays only increased Mordecai's power. Yet, Mordecai did not appeal to Yahweh, nor was he depicted as being a follower of Yahweh.

In Esther 4:14 Mordecai made the well-known statement to Esther, "For if you remain silent at this time, relief and deliverance will arise for the Jews from another place and you and your father's house will perish. And who knows whether you have attained royalty for such a time as this?"

This initially sounds like a God-fearing statement, but upon closer inspection, it makes no mention of God. Mordecai believed the people of Israel would be delivered, but he did not say why he had that hope or tell the basis of his expectation.

Esther was depicted in the same way. After King Ahasuerus rejected Vashti as queen, he put on a royal pageant to choose his next bride. Esther, whether willingly or unwillingly, was in this pageant. She hid her Jewish identity, concealing any hint that she might be a follower of Yahweh. Whether she was a follower of Yahweh or not, she was ashamed at first to be called a Jewess.

We often place Ruth and Esther into a similar category, but that was not the intention of the Scriptures. Ruth was certainly understood as being a godly woman who proclaimed that, even though she was a Moabitess, she would follow Yahweh faithfully.

But Esther, even though she was a Jewess, did not mention one word about Yahweh. Esther was exalted to power, and God used her to deliver the people of Israel from destruction, but it was not because Esther was depicted as being a godly woman.

Just as with the rest of the Old Testament, Yahweh was the One who was righteous, faithful, and good. He worked through many different types of characters in the Old Testament to bring about His purposes. He demonstrated His loyal covenant love through the Noahic, Abrahamic, Mosaic, and Davidic covenants, pointing to the One who is to come who will be the true Seed of Abraham, who will sit on David's throne as King, judging in righteousness.

Study Questions:

1. Why would the author of Esther take the time to create such an intricate structure?

2. Why was God's name never mentioned in Esther?

3. What was the connection between Haman and King Saul?

4. What was at the center of the book of Esther?

5. What did the center of the book of Esther tell us about God's sovereignty?

6. Do you think that Esther and Mordecai were godly examples or not? Why?